HARVARD EAST ASIAN MONOGRAPHS
38

JAMES DUNCAN CAMPBELL

A MEMOIR BY HIS SON

JAMES DUNCAN CAMPBELL

A MEMOIR BY HIS SON

by
Robert Ronald Campbell
Christ Church, Oxford, M. A.
Lincoln's Inn, Barrister-at-Law

Published by
East Asian Research Center
Harvard University

Distributed by
Harvard University Press
Cambridge, Mass.
1970

Copyright, 1970, by

the President and Fellows of

Harvard College

The East Asian Research Center at Harvard University
administers research projects designed to further
scholarly understanding of China, Japan, Korea, Vietnam,
and adjacent areas. These studies have been assisted by
grants from the Ford Foundation.

Library of Congress No. 72-123565
SBN 674-47131-8

*Taking him all round, his character and his
career, he was rather an illustration of the
bitter saying, "that the world knows nothing
of its greatest men."*

Paul King

*He had but one honourable defect. He was
modest and retiring to a fault.*

Lord Stuart Rendel

CONTENTS

FOREWORD

The East Asian Research Center is preparing for publication the unusual series of more than a thousand confidential letters written by Sir Robert Hart as head of the Chinese Imperial Maritime Customs Service to his London agent, James Duncan Campbell. This Hart-to-Campbell correspondence continued from 1868 to 1907 and touched upon myriad things of importance in China's foreign relations. Hart was a great figure in China throughout this period. Who was Campbell?

We are fortunate to have received from Mr. L. K. Little (who was Hart's eventual successor as Inspector General in the years 1943 to 1950) a copy of the "first typewritten draft" of a memoir of Campbell written by his son, Robert R. Campbell. The draft had been completed in 1944 and 1945 and the copy of it sent to Mr. Little as I. G. about 1947. By the time we saw it, along with the Hart letters, in 1969 and realized the value of the memoir, we found that Mr. R. R. Campbell had died in 1961, and that three appendices to which his memoir refers had not been sent with it to Mr. Little and appear now to have been destroyed after his death. These three appendices were planned by the author to consist of extracts of letters written by James Duncan Campbell, extracts of letters to Campbell from friends in China, and a translation of a Tsungli Yamen memorial conferring honors on Hart and Campbell for their part in the negotiation of the Sino-French treaty of 1885. The little evidence available to us indicates that these materials and others on which the son relied in writing of his father have all suffered inadvertent destruction.

The editorial problem thus created, to prepare for publication the draft of an author now deceased, has been dealt with by Mrs. Elizabeth MacLeod Matheson, whose patient and fruitful work for this Center during the last two decades may be likened in a minor way to that of James Duncan Campbell for the Customs—self-effacing, scrupulously efficient, and essential. Mrs. Matheson has corrected obvious errors of spelling, dating, and the like, and in the process has regularized romanizations and checked many references.

Many of the original documents used by the author have not been available to us, but the memoir, which is written with liveliness and presents interesting details over a wide range of subjects, seems to us to deserve publication for the use of historians. We are indebted to Mrs. R. R. Campbell for permission to publish and to Mr. Little for his Introduction.

John K. Fairbank

June 1970

INTRODUCTION

James Duncan Campbell was the prototype of the very finest civil servant. Appointed to the infant Chinese Customs Service in 1862, he was on leave of absence in England in 1870 when his chief, Robert Hart, Inspector General of the Chinese Customs, asked him to manage an appeal that Hart had before the Privy Council. The appeal sought to reverse a decision against Hart that had been made in Shanghai by a British consular court.

On the successful outcome of this appeal, Hart found other tasks for Campbell in England, and after some initial hesitation he decided to have a permanent representative in Europe. He told Campbell that he wanted for the position "a man who knows China as you do . . . a man thoroughly trusted by me as you are and personally loyal to me as I believe you to be." As the obvious choice, Campbell opened the London office of the Chinese Customs Service in 1873 and was given the rather odd-sounding title of "non-resident secretary" (indicating that he was an inspectorate secretary not residing in China).

From 1873 until his death in 1907 Campbell served as Hart's representative and alter ego in Europe. As this memoir by his son, the late Mr. Robert Ronald Campbell, amply shows, Hart made Campbell responsible for the expenditure of millions of pounds in procuring ships, lighthouses, and countless other supplies for the Customs. It was also Campbell's duty to examine European candidates for the Customs Service, and on several occasions Hart assigned to him important diplomatic missions. Hart also entrusted him with the investment of his private funds and the often delicate task of dealing with members of his immediate family and some more distant relatives.

Mr. Campbell tells of his father's leading role as Hart's representative in the negotiations that ended the war between China and France, and in the negotiations with the Portuguese government over the status of Macao. In both cases Campbell acted with perspicacity, skill, and patience, and much of the credit for the successful outcome of these ventures in diplomacy should be given to him. In *Hart and the Chinese Customs* Stanley F. Wright says, "In fact, without Campbell's loyalty, ability and tact, Hart could not have carried out either of these diplomatic successes."

Hart, who was inclined to be sparing in praise of his subordinates, did occasionally express his satisfaction with Campbell's work. As early as 1876 he wrote, "You do your work uncommonly well, and it is a great satisfaction to me to know that I have such a reliable man in England."

The Inspector General allowed himself no intimates in Peking and had the reputation of being somewhat aloof even with his close associates. In one of his letters to Campbell he wrote, "The worst of it is I am utterly alone and have not a single friend or confidant—man, woman or child." And yet to Campbell he opened his heart and confided his most intimate thoughts and feelings. The relationship between Hart and Campbell—who met only two or three times in thirty-four years—became more like that of brothers or close friends than chief and subordinate, and Campbell's death in 1907 left Hart lonely and bereft.

A voluminous official correspondence passed between Peking and London; in addition, Campbell and Hart wrote privately to each other almost every week. These letters are remarkably candid in their comments on current events and personalities, both Chinese and foreign. The author of the memoir writes, "Should these letters . . . ever be published to the world, they would certainly yield an interesting picture of Chinese and European history from 1874 to 1907."

Hart's private letters to Campbell have been preserved and are now being edited for eventual publication by the Harvard University Press. Campbell's letters to Hart were destroyed during the Boxer Rebellion, but Campbell had kept copies of his letters in press-copy books. These were sent from London to the Inspectorate General of Customs in Shanghai in 1947 and it is to be hoped that they have been preserved by the present Customs administration.

This memoir contains material of interest to students of Chinese history during the last third of the nineteenth century, especially with regard to the development of the unique Customs Service and the kind of men who made it such a useful institution. It is, however, first and foremost a filial tribute to a man who brought credit on his family and his own country and served

China and his distant chief for forty-four years with skill, loyalty, integrity, and modesty.

L. K. Little
Inspector General
Chinese Customs Service
1943-1950

June 1970

AUTHOR'S PREFACE

When going through my father's papers after his death in December 1907, I discovered a number of documents and letters relating to China. These I collected and arranged in bundles, in the hope that, should I or anyone else attempt subsequently to write his memoirs, they would prove to be useful. For certainly his career seemed sufficiently unique to merit some sort of permanent record. For years I did nothing. But when Lord Stuart Rendel's memoirs were published in 1931,[*] containing an entirely erroneous account of the part my father had played in the negotiations which led to the termination of the war between France and China in 1885, I felt that the time had come to do something. After writing to Lord Rendel's executors and getting them to insert an apologetic letter in the *Times*, I set seriously to work. So many interruptions occurred, however, that I could only tackle the task at long intervals, and it is only now (in the 1940s) that I have been able to complete this draft.

In the meantime two books were published in which some slight reference was made to Campbell's work. The first, entitled *Sir Robert Hart*, was written by his niece Juliet Bredon and published by Hutchinson and Co. in 1909. I was so much annoyed by the way in which the writer had belittled my father's services that I sent her a strong remonstrance, but on the advice of Sir Robert, who was still alive at the time, I refrained from taking further action. The second was Paul King's *In the Chinese Customs Service*, published by Fisher Unwin in 1924. King had served for some years in London under my father and therefore knew something of the work he had done, and he eventually succeeded himself to the post which my father had once occupied. His book closes with a short appreciation of Campbell's work, which I think so charming that I give here the main portions of it:

> For those who knew him and appreciated his self-sacrificing labours Mr Campbell's record stands fast. He was naturally a great deal in my thoughts, and sitting in his chair I often seemed to hear his hurried footsteps coming up the stairs. I was, of course, well acquainted with all the work—official and private—he did for the great I. G. Did he get the fruits

---

*Lord Stuart Rendel, *The Personal Papers of Lord Rendel* (London: E. Benn Ltd., 1931).

of his labours even in the complimentary sense of recognition of those services at the hands of his Chief? I trow not. Robert Hart was essentially ungenerous in this respect and stood for the idea, "Alone I did it," and this attitude of mind could never admit the existence of an assistant, lest haply the world should doubt his own omniscience. He had one opportunity at least in London of paying a tribute to Campbell's memory but failed to do so.

Campbell's work was to a great extent confidential and between him and his Chief alone. The Service knew little and the Public nothing of it. He never claimed any credit or recognition, but effaced himself with the loyalty of his Highland blood. All the more reason that the man who did know should have spoken. Campbell predeceased the I. G. He worked on to the last, and his faithful service ended only with his death in 1907.

What little I could do to perpetuate in the London Office the memory of its most distinguished occupant I did, in getting a very fine enlargement of his photograph in Court Dress, wearing the insignia of the Chinese Double Dragon, and the C. M. G. conferred on him by his own Sovereign. It hangs on the wall of the Secretary's room at 26, Old Queen Street, looking down on the Chair he occupied for thirty-five eventful years— a record which in the nature of things can never be beaten. Mr Campbell bore a remarkable resemblance to the late Lord Salisbury, and was often mistaken for that eminent Statesman during his daily walk over the bridge in St James's Park to luncheon at the Thatched House Club in St James's Street . . .

Personally I owe him much. He possessed an unrivalled (in the Customs Service) despatch style, and had besides a wonderful knowledge of official account-keeping. His diplomatic talents were of a high order, and he had a large share of insight and even "second sight," added to excellent judgment. I was with him so much at various periods that I should have been a dull ass indeed if I had not absorbed at least something from his ever kindly teachings. His praise ought to have been sung by loftier harps than mine, but as it was not I venture to add a lowly tribute to his many virtues and remarkable qualities of efficiency, self-abnegation and fidelity. Taking him all round, his character and his career, he was rather an illustration of the bitter saying, "that the world knows nothing of its greatest men." Certainly lesser men were better known than James Duncan Campbell and reaped rewards far beyond their deserts, but not beyond his![*]

*King, pp. 296-298.

Campbell's China career covered practically the whole of the last half-century of Manchu rule, and the prominent position which he occupied immediately under Sir Robert Hart naturally brought him into close touch with most of the big events of that period. Indeed this memoir may be said to constitute a history in miniature of China, and in particular of the Customs Service during these years. What a fine service it was, the Chinese Imperial Maritime Customs, under its great Inspector General, Sir Robert Hart! In a vast country (inhabited by some 400 millions of the human race) notorious for the bribery and corruption of the official classes, it shone out incorruptible like a beacon of pure light until, as port after port was opened to foreign trade and its sphere of activities gradually increased, there were few places where you could not truthfully say, "Here the Customs Service did good." Much of the admirable work it did for China and the world is already well known: its wise and careful administration of the Customs which gave to China a sure and ever-increasing revenue, on the security of which she found no difficulty in raising numerous loans; its gradual lighting of China's eighteen hundred miles of coast line which made that coast, in the opinion of many, the best lighted in the world; its establishment of an imperial postal service, and so on.

Not so well known are numerous other extraordinary activities, conducted mainly by Hart and Campbell. How few there are, for example, who know that, mainly through the instrumentality of Campbell, China acquired a fleet which for a short time was the most powerful in the Pacific and effectually curbed the evil machinations of Japan. The full story of the building of this fleet is given herein, along with extracts from several letters written to Campbell by Admiral William M. Lang and expressing his high opinion of the fleet. If only China had been wise enough to entrust the administration of this fleet to the Customs Service, as Lang recommended, how different might have been the history of the East! How few there are, again, who know that the great Inspector General on at least one occasion became practically China's foreign minister. The full story of the secret negotiations conducted in Paris in 1885, which brought to an end the war between China and France, and incidentally saved a European conflict, is told below. Also recorded is Hart's amazing prophecy of the ultimate aims of Japan and his vain attempt, at the end of the Sino-Japanese War, to induce Great Britain to form an alliance with China instead of with Japan; and here, for the first time, is the true story of how the memorial service at Saint Paul's Cathedral, for those who were supposed to have been massacred at Peking during the Boxer Rising, was put off.

This memoir indeed amounts to something considerably more than a personal history of Campbell. Together with the extracts from letters given in the appendices,[**] it throws an interesting light on the general history of China during a very eventful period.

Sir Robert Hart looms large in these pages. Considering the long and intimate relationship which prevailed between the two men, it could not be otherwise. There can be absolutely no doubt he was a wonderful man. True, he had his enemies who complained, sometimes bitterly, of the harshness of his autocratic rule, of his unkindness and unfairness in keeping the services of others in the background, and of the favouritism which he displayed to members of his own and his wife's family. But what great man has not his faults? And even Hart's worst enemies admitted his amazing abilities and admired his fortitude at the time of the Boxer Rising and the philosophic calm with which he bore disappointment and loss. King's "Pen Portrait of Sir Robert Hart, the Great I. G."[*] is the best description of him I have come across, but King had been rather roughly treated by Hart at times and in consequence was perhaps a little hard on him. As for my father, hurt though he undoubtedly was at his own services never being openly recognized, Hart always seeking to obtain the whole credit for himself, he nevertheless maintained always a genuine admiration and a warm affection for Hart and would never allow a word to be said against him. He summed up his character in these parting words to my brother when the latter left England to join Hart in Peking, in the spring of 1892. "Remember," he said, "Sir Robert has two sides, the official and the private. As an official he is stern and relentless and expects hard work and loyalty. Do your level best and serve him loyally, and then, when the working day is over, you will find him in private the kindest and most considerate of friends."

*King, chap. 20.
**Re appendices, see Foreword.

It is not for me, who knew Hart only on paper, to express an opinion on him, but certain things impressed me as I went through all the papers. The first was the transparent genius of the man, the second was kindliness and generosity shown on many an occasion, and the third was his dry sense of Irish humour. How, for example, beat this taken from a letter written by his chief secretary in Peking on 21 March 1876: "Mrs Hart left here on Sunday last and the I. G. amused himself on the very day of her departure in elaborating an edict against matrimony."

That my father's affection for Hart was reciprocated is shown, I think, by the touching letters he wrote to my mother and myself after my father's death. He was deeply distressed at the loss of his old friend, and life could no longer be the same for him. He left China shortly afterwards and lived a little longer in loneliness here in England, deprived, as he himself wrote to me, "of the talks which we should have had about the multitudinous matters in which we had both been so much concerned and so much in communication." This to him was perhaps his greatest grief, not to be able to see my father. But the talks for which he yearned have now doubtless been long since held in the Great Beyond.

R. R. Campbell

England
February 1944

CAMPBELL'S EARLY YEARS, 1833-1853

James Duncan Campbell was born at 7 Warriston Crescent, Edinburgh, on 9 February 1833. His father, Major Robert Campbell, of the Forty-sixth Regiment, was the second son of James Campbell, younger of Craignish, a famous old West Highland family. His mother Louisa was the daughter of David Baillie, a Scot who had acquired considerable wealth in Jamaica and on his death in 1826 had left the bulk of his fortune between this Louisa and her brother, the Reverend Jasper Baillie.

James Duncan was the first-born of this marriage; he was a seven-months child and so small at birth that, as he used often laughingly to relate, he had his early washings in a soup tureen. Shortly after his birth, his father's regiment was sent to Gibraltar, and here James Duncan spent his earliest years. When about five years of age he came over to England by sea, travelling by himself, to be looked after by his uncle Jasper Baillie, then vicar of Great Rissington in Gloucestershire. Though his uncle was very strict, he was also exceedingly kind; he ultimately bequeathed to him his fortune of some £30,000.

Sometime after this the Forty-sixth was moved to Ireland, and it is in Ireland that his father and mother were stationed when his mother's most interesting diary begins in 1843. At the beginning of 1845 James, whom we shall now call Campbell, left his uncle's care and was sent to Cheltenham College. He did well both as a student and in sports; he was in the cricket eleven from 1848 to 1850 and gained a devotion for the game which never left him. Indeed, one of the few relaxations which he allowed himself in a strenuous official life, during which he scarcely took any leave, was a day or afternoon at Kennington Oval, of which he was a member. In classics he became so sound a scholar that his masters wished him to compete for a Balliol scholarship. His father and mother were with the regiment in Canada during his first three years at Cheltenham. They returned in 1848, and we find Campbell spending the summer holidays of this year with the regiment at Dover Castle. A little later his father sold out his army commission, and Campbell's holidays were then spent in Edinburgh, where his parents went to live. One of his chief friends at Cheltenham, though slightly his senior, was Henry James, who later became Lord Chancellor James of Hereford. Campbell maintained the closest relations with him in after life, retaining him as chief English counsel when the question of the rightful heir to Craignish arose in 1875.

When Campbell left Cheltenham his father gave him the option of going to Balliol or studying abroad. He chose the latter, spending the years 1851 and 1852 at Boulogne and Paris, and 1853 at Heidelberg University. I find among the papers of this time a testimonial from Dr Hobson, principal of Cheltenham College, who was quick to notice a trait in his character—an excessive modesty—which he never succeeded entirely in shaking off. Dr Hobson wrote of him in October 1850:

> Mr James Duncan Campbell was under my care and instruction at Cheltenham College for the space of nearly six years. During the whole of this period his conduct was in every respect entirely unexceptionable. I believe I can say with truth that while he was under my immediate charge, I never received from any master with whom he was concerned a complaint of any kind respecting him; while I have heard favourable opinions expressed of him by all. And for nearly a year he was in the first class of the school which is taught immediately by myself. I found him at all times what his previous conduct would have led me to expect. Possessed of very fair abilities much improved by attention and application, he was also modest, docile and unassuming, and rather, I think, inclined to underrate his own powers than the contrary. In his course through life, I feel sure, that supposing him to continue what I ever knew him, he cannot fail to ensure the respect and esteem of all with whom he may come in contact.

Whether Campbell was wise in abandoning an Oxford career may be doubted, but he certainly gained a knowledge of French which was exceedingly useful to him later in his dealings with the French government, particularly when negotiating the treaty between France and China in 1885. As to Heidelberg, though he forgot most of his German, he used to look back to his university days there with the fondest memory. I remember that in the nineties a play called *Old Heidelberg* was produced in London by Sir George Alexander; he and I went, and I watched with sympathy the tears running down his face as he recalled the sparkling days of youth.

CAMPBELL IN THE BRITISH CIVIL SERVICE, 1856-1862

At the end of 1853, his course at Heidelberg finished, Campbell left for India to join his youngest uncle Smollett Campbell, who was a merchant in Calcutta. The Suez Canal was not yet opened and he travelled via the Cape. Any idea he may have had of a business career in India was soon dispelled, however, for he had not been more than a few months in Calcutta when his uncle died of cholera, and he had the melancholy task of bringing the widow and her three children back to England. He stayed a short time with his father and mother at Bath, played a certain amount of cricket with his friends the Graces, and then proceeded to Germany to renew his German studies.

Returning to England at the beginning of 1855, he studied under Dr Wilkinson, formerly Fellow of Clare College, Cambridge, with a view to competing for the Indian Civil Service. When the time came for the examination, however, he was found to be above the age limit, and his mother's diary shows that he and his parents were becoming disturbed as to his future. Another disappointment was to follow. The Crimean War was now raging, and letters were written to Sir Colin Campbell, whose mother was of Craignish descent, and to General Peter Campbell, a cousin on the Duntroon side, asking them to use their influence to obtain a commission for him. But once again he was found to be too old. The Duke of Argyll, who at that time was postmaster general, was then approached, and success came at last, for the duke at once (February 1856) nominated him to a vacancy in the Post Office. Continuing to take a personal interest in him as a scion of Craignish, the duke later arranged for him to compete for a vacancy in the Treasury. Out of several strong candidates he obtained first place in the examination and joined the Treasury in August 1856. The duke, though he had countenanced the idea, seems nevertheless to have been a little annoyed at his leaving the Post Office so soon. In November 1856 he wrote to Major Robert Campbell: "I regret very much that he has left the P.O. From what I have heard of your son, I feel sure that he would have advanced readily in the P.O. He has left an excellent impression behind him in the Office of his abilities and character."

At the Treasury Campbell speedily made his mark, and shortly after his advent he became secretary to Sir Charles E. Trevelyan, its chief. He had been there a little over eighteen months when he was promoted to the Audit Office, being again chosen first after competition. His mother's diary reveals that he was warmly complimented by Trevelyan, who presented him with a book written by himself. While he was at the Audit Office he took an active part in the volunteer movement, which by 1859 had become a great national organisation, and he earned a considerable reputation for military enthusiasm and efficiency. He became lieutenant of the Audit Office company and musketry instructor to the whole body of the Civil Service volunteers.

Towards the end of 1862 Campbell left the Civil Service to take an appointment in the Chinese Customs Service. His seven years in the Post Office and the Treasury had been enjoyable, and the fine training he had received was undoubtedly of immense value when it fell to him a little later to establish a system of accounts for his new Service and to organise the office machinery not only for its London office but for the various Customs offices throughout China.

III

CAMPBELL IN CHINA, 1863-1870

In April 1861 Mr Horatio Nelson Lay, the first Inspector General of the Chinese Imperial Maritime Customs, left for England on sick leave after having been nearly done to death by a Chinese miscreant in Shanghai. The Customs Service, which later was destined to discharge such important functions for China, political as well as administrative, was then in its infancy. It owed its origin to the gradual opening of treaty ports to foreign trade. Before the war of 1840 with Great Britain, the only Chinese port where Europeans were allowed to trade was Canton; one result of that war had been the opening of the additional ports of Amoy, Foochow, Ningpo, and Shanghai. Initially, the British consuls assisted in the administration of the customs in the ports, but in 1851 they ceased to do so and confusion followed until 1854.

In that year the Chinese superintendent of customs at Shanghai, which was then in the hands of the Triad rebels, found the task of collecting the duties so bewildering and difficult that he appealed to the consuls of Britain, France, and the United States for help. The result was the appointment of a triumvirate of foreign customs inspectors, consisting of one representative from each of these countries. Mr Thomas F. Wade (later Sir Thomas) was the British representative. By 1855, however, all three had resigned, and Mr Lay, an expert Chinese linguist and the British vice-consul at Shanghai, was appointed to the post of foreign inspector and henceforward managed things alone. This new administration at Shanghai was found to be so honest, efficient, and profitable to the Chinese government that its sphere of activities was extended after 1858-1860; the opening of still further treaty ports after the Tientsin Treaty (arranged by Lord Elgin in 1858 and ratified in 1860) necessarily involved additions to the inspectorate staff.

Foreigners had by now been permitted to aid in the administration as officials of the Chinese government, and one of Mr Lay's first tasks on arriving in England was to find an expert British official to help him in his work. His choice fell on Campbell, who was strongly backed by Sir Charles Trevelyan, head of the Treasury. It required no little courage for Campbell to accept the offer, for it meant throwing up a promising career in the Treasury for a post under a foreign government which in those days could not be regarded as a permanent certainty. It was an adventure, however, full of possibilities, which appealed to his Highland spirit; he took the plunge, resigned from the Treasury, and on 1 December 1862 reported for duty at the office of the Chinese Customs' agent in London.

Campbell's resignation from the Treasury occasioned considerable regret among the Civil Service volunteers for whom he had done such valuable work. At a recent distribution of prizes to the Civil Service company, Lord Bury had spoken highly of his services as musketry instructor, and the *Telegraph Newspaper* of 14 November 1862 reported that when he came forward to receive his prize of a handsome cigar case "three thundering cheers greeted his appearance." Lord Bury himself wrote a long letter of appreciation which ended: "If the Chief of the Chinese expedition knew you as well as I do he would not hesitate to secure you. I speak very confidently, for, as Colonel of the Regiment in which you have filled a very arduous post, I have watched your conduct closely and admiringly." Captain Hawkes, his company commander, wrote:

> I cannot sufficiently express to you, my dear Campbell, the very sincere regret that I feel, and that every member of my Company feels, at losing one whom they have had every reason to like so much and to be so proud of. There is not an officer of the Regiment who has devoted himself so zealously and so successfully for the advantage of the Corps as yourself. Personally as your Captain I shall feel your loss most sincerely in every way, and I cannot but express to you my best acknowledgments of the great services you have rendered the Company and myself, and for the valuable advice which you have always been ready to offer in so modest a manner, and which, I can assure you, will never be forgotten by me.

Campbell was much gratified by these marks of esteem. It had always been a sore point with him that he had not been a soldier like his forebears. His father and his ancestors for five generations back had all been in the army and he was the first to break the military traditions of the Craignish family. It was, therefore, some slight consolation to him to know that the hard work he had put in as one of the pioneers of the volunteer movement was appreciated.

One of the first things Campbell did on receiving his appointment was to make a close study of the various trade treaties with China and to gain some knowledge of Chinese history. He realised that for a foreigner to administer well in a strange land it was essential to know something of the people and their past. The ordinary Englishman of those days was strangely ignorant of China and of everything Chinese. Chinese history was not taught in the schools; perhaps this was because, apart from a slight trade in silk, China had never come into contact with the Roman Empire; also, apart from a doubtful reference to the Land of Sinim in Isaiah 49:12, China is not mentioned in the Bible. It was not, therefore, considered an appropriate subject for inclusion in the school curriculum.

The ordinary man's idea of China was that it was a semibarbaric country, not fit to be treated like the civilised nations of Europe. Few realised that, at a time when the so-called civilised nations were mere savages, China had a wonderful civilisation almost as old as that of ancient Egypt, under which it was possible not only to live but to live well; that, as Cobden pointed out when protesting in the House of Commons against England's behaviour towards China in 1856-1858 over the *Arrow* incident, "it had its Logic before Aristotle, and a philosophy before Socrates." Few were aware that its people had many charming characteristics and that its art was superb. As the years went by, Campbell learnt to know the people well and acquired a love and respect for them which enabled him to sympathise with them to the full in their numerous troubles and difficulties.

His post under Mr Lay was that of chief secretary and auditor and he left for China with Mr Lay in March 1863. From the time he left Campbell kept a careful journal which he sent home regularly. This and his letters for this period have unfortunately been lost, and I am dependent on his mother's diary for particulars of his first voyage to China. From this we learn that it took him six weeks and four days to reach Shanghai. The itinerary is of interest to us in these days of speedy air travel. He left Marseilles on 28 March, reached Malta on the thirtieth, Alexandria on 3 April, Suez (by rail) the fourth, Aden the ninth, Ceylon the eighteenth, Singapore the twenty-ninth, Hongkong on 5 May, and Shanghai the thirteenth. He left Shanghai by an uncomfortable tug steamer on 23 May, reached Tientsin on the twenty-ninth, and was in Peking, his journey's end, by the beginning of June 1863.

At the time of his arrival the vast empire of China was passing through a serious crisis. The territory north of the Amur and east of the Ussuri had recently been ceded to Russia, which had also founded the port of Vladivostok; in the south, France, having occupied Cochin China and Cambodia, was encroaching on the Chinese vassal state of Annam; and the Taiping Rebellion was still in full swing. Moreover, the imperial house was only just recovering from the indignity of the march of the British and French forces to Peking and the burning of the Summer Palace (1860). There had been confusion in the royal household. The Hsien-feng Emperor (1851-1861), who had fled from Peking before the allies entered, had died in Jehol, and his successor, his only son the T'ung-chih Emperor, was a boy only five years of age. There had been a violent quarrel as to the regency, and it was China's misfortune that boy emperors were henceforward to be the rule, for another boy, the Kuang-hsü Emperor, succeeded in 1875, and still another boy, Pu-yi, the Hsuan-t'ung Emperor, in 1909. Unhappy nearly always has been the fate of countries with boy emperors or kings, and perhaps this was one of the causes which contributed to the fall of the Manchu dynasty in 1911 after it had held sway for some 250 years.

The real power at the time of Campbell's arrival was in the hands of the two dowager empresses, of whom Tz'u-hsi, the emperor's mother, afterwards known as "Old Buddha," and one of the most remarkable women the world has ever known, was by far the stronger. The other, Tz'u-an, though the senior, was childless and weak. It is curious that a woman should have attained such power in the East, where the position of women is as a rule much inferior to that of men, but there is no doubt that Tz'u-hsi was an extraordinary woman, and her ability and courage had recently been shown in crushing a serious conspiracy. The two empresses were assisted by the late emperor's brothers, of whom Prince Kung, "the sixth prince," and Prince Ch'un, "the seventh prince," were the most conspicuous, the former being president of the Tsungli Yamen (the Chinese foreign office). Li Hung-chang, later to be for so long viceroy of Chihli, was also a power in the land.

Campbell's initial stay in Peking was of only short duration. Trouble arose with regard to the gunboat fleet which Mr Lay had recently been instructed to purchase. Captain Sherard Osborn, the British naval officer in command of the fleet (he had been lent by the British Admiralty) quarrelled with the authorities and declined to continue in China. The result of it all was that the fleet was ordered to be returned to England, to be sold. Mr Lay and Campbell returned with it, presumably to conduct the sale. The failure of the fleet was a bad business, and at the time it was thought by the British and American ministers in Peking and by others that it was likely to be followed by the total breakup of the Customs Service. Campbell's mother's diary shows that he left Peking on 12 November 1863, picked up the fleet at Shanghai, and then travelled with it via the Cape, his vessel being the *China*, commanded by Commander Osborn, Captain Sherard Osborn's brother. Other vessels were the *Peking*, the *Tientsin*, and the *Scout*. He landed at Deal in April 1864 and for the next few months was busily engaged with Mr Lay in London. It appears from his mother's diary that he had some "annoyances" with Mr Lay, but what they were is not disclosed.

In July a great misfortune befell him, which rendered him *hors de combat* for nearly two years. He was out with his old company of volunteers at Wimbledon when, in jumping a fence, he alighted on a stone and broke his thigh in two places. He was under the care of English doctors for all the rest of 1864, but they bungled the job, and to make matters worse a serious illness followed. He was subsequently advised to consult a famous French surgeon, Dr Paquet, and for practically the whole of 1865 and the early part of 1866 he was in France undergoing treatment in Paris, Roubaix, and Lille. Ultimately the thigh mended, but for the rest of his life one leg was shorter than the other and he had to wear special boots made for him by the famous firm of Thomas in Saint James's Street. He was never afterwards able to play games properly or walk much, and his peculiar walk earned for him among his friends the nickname of "Dot and go one."

Meanwhile Mr Lay had been given his *congé* by the Chinese government, which was thought rather an injustice at the time, and Robert Hart, who had joined the Customs Service in 1859 as deputy commissioner at Canton, had stepped into his shoes. Rumour had it that Hart had ingratiated himself with the Chinese during Lay's absence and undermined his position. The truth probably is that the Chinese government, rightly or wrongly, was annoyed with Lay for the failure of the gunboat fleet and at the same time considered Hart the abler man. What Campbell's position was during all these happenings is not clear, but he had much correspondence with Hart, and when the latter came to England in 1866 for a much needed rest he lost no time in appointing Campbell, now fully recovered from his illness, to his old post as chief secretary. His salary was £1200 a year, which was increased as the years went on to £1600, £2000, and finally £2500.

In September 1866 Campbell returned to China with Hart and the latter's newly wedded wife, and his mother's diary gives a sorrowful account of his farewell talk with his uncle Jasper Baillie, now a dying man. The entry reads: "13 Sept. Dearest James left this morning . . . I feel wretched. The nurse said my brother cried very much at parting with him and prayed for him. May his prayers be heard." A batch of letters written to his father and mother gave an interesting account of this his second voyage to the East. In addition to the Harts were several passengers of all nationalities, including some Dutch damsels with whom the menfolk speedily fell in love. Also included was Johannes von Gumpach, a German whom Hart had appointed as one of the professors at his new college in Peking. Von Gumpach, despite his middle age and to the amusement of everyone, became involved in some love affairs and even at that date gave signs of a temperament which later led to a serious quarrel between him and Hart and ultimately to an expensive lawsuit fought first in Shanghai and then before the Privy Council in London. One of the Frenchmen on board, Baron de Martens, who was a good Chinese scholar, gave lessons in Chinese of which Campbell took assiduous advantage. On 13 October 1866 he wrote from Point de Galles:

> I have been studying Chinese every day, and have made such progress that I am long way ahead of all the others, so much so that I alone receive instruction from the Baron, and the others not being able to keep up with me, prefer from necessity to work and study separately and alone. I have learnt about 70 of the radicals, and over 100 characters, and I hope, before reaching Peking, to have the 214 radicals at my fingers' ends and to know about 500 characters. It is a pity that I shall have but little time to give to the study of the language on my arrival. I expect for the first two or three months to be very busy, as there will be all the arrears of the last 8 or 9 months to get through—arrears owing to Mr. Hart's absence.

Another Frenchman, M. Kelsch, the baron's friend, became very friendly. Campbell wrote of him:

He is going to Peking under the auspices of the French Government
to endeavour to have a camp of instruction at Peking. He sits next to
me at the second mess and we have become great cronies. He has had
a very adventurous life; yesterday was his birthday when he was 44
years old. He says he has had several happy days in his life and many
sorrowful years, so I wished him few sorrowful days to come and many
happy years. He was one of the youngest captains in the French Army
at the age of 24, when he unfortunately dabbled in politics and commenced by taking command of a volunteer Italian regiment in the war
against Austria. He had the command of the left bank of the Seine and
fought at the barricades at the coup d'etat of 1851. He afterwards tried
to upset Louis Napoleon's Govt and was shot through the top of the
head. However, he is now good friends with the Emperor and a partisan
of the Govt. Had he known or imagined what would have been the future
conduct of the Emperor and the nature of his Govt he would have been
the last to oppose him.

The Dutch damsels got off at Singapore, much to Campbell's relief. A duel
between a Frenchman and an Englishman of Tientsin, in which one of the
girls was involved, had only narrowly been averted by his intervention. The
voyage was a fairly short one for those times, but it was not till the end of
November that the travellers reached Peking, doing the last part of the
journey on land, as the frost had set in and the river was frozen.

Campbell's first year after his return to Peking was a busy one and his
work brought him constantly into touch with Prince Kung, the sixth son of
the Tao-kuang Emperor and still the most important man in China. His portrait in a handsome frame used to hang in our drawing room at Clanricarde
Gardens and I still have it. Hart soon formed the highest opinion of Campbell's
capabilities and whenever there was a difficult piece of work to do entrusted
it to his care. At the end of 1867, for example, Hart sent him on a special
mission to Japan, to settle some difficulty which had arisen with the Japanese
government. His mother's diary shows that he wrote home regularly each
week, and I give here extracts from some of the letters which have been
preserved:

11 Feb. 1867. Mr. Hart called today at the Foreign Office. He went
in his Chinese robes to meet Prince Kung, and on his return he sent for
me to give me a surprise. He saluted me in Chinese fashion and for a
second or so I did not recognise him. He wore a magnificent sable coat

with the beads and other paraphernalia of his rank, presented him by
the Chinese Govt and worth several hundred pounds.

12 Feb. 1867 [The new college was not doing too well]. Altogether
it has been a bad commencement of the College, and I think Mr Hart
is a little disgusted with the turn matters have taken. He called upon the
Professors to report to him what they thought should be the course of
study for 5 years in their respective Departments. Von Gumpach made
a very elaborate report, asking for great things, an observatory, etc.
I expect Mr Hart will have some trouble with him, but I warned him of
this in England before he made the appointment.

I have a great deal of work to do, and what with my Chinese studies,
I have no time for diversion. The Chinese New Year commenced the 5th
of the month, and they have been letting off fireworks ever since. The
report was spread again that all the foreigners were to be massacred on
the second night, but I slept without thinking or dreaming of it. I expect
there will be fighting in Corea in the Spring. I hope the English will not
allow the French to have it all to themselves.

I am far ahead of all of them in Chinese at present and have devised a
scheme for the study of the radicals and characters, which is pronounced
by all as excellent. Von Gumpach himself has taken up the idea. Unhappily I have not the time to study properly.

At present everything is going on very well, I think I have Mr Hart's
confidence and he has mine—but one has to be extraordinarily careful
both in words and deeds. A word uttered accidentally may be turned
into a sentence, and the sentence into a history, so that one may be
reported to say what never existed in his mind. I am becoming taciturn
and reticent, but it is both prudent and necessary.

I have written to Mr Stephenson again this mail about the gas. [Gas
was being introduced into Peking.] The Chinese have asked Mr Hart
many questions about it, but they appear to have a curious interest in
the experiment. Its success will depend entirely upon the gas-giving
properties of the coal in the neighbourhood—but a cargo of good English
coal has been shipped, so that, in the first instance, there may be no
failure.

21 March 1867 [Even in these early days he thought highly of
Hart]. Mr Hart has his hands full of work and it is astonishing how easily
he gets through it all. He is a wonderful clear-headed far-seeing man, and
writes with force, judgment and Perspicuity.

25 April 1867. We are to have a new French Minister here, the Count de Lalemont, who comes out as an Ambassador and is therefore higher in rank than other Ministers. He has commenced work, on dit, already in Canton, for the formation of a Franco-Chinese naval force. If anything of the kind takes place, I think it will be in connection with the Customs and under Hart.

9 May 1867. Mr Hart has bought houses for the Professors, who will move into them as soon as possible.

31 July 1867 [He did not like Peking in those days]. What a dismal place is Peking! ruin and desolation everywhere, squalor and nakedness, misery and poverty! No amusement, no society, no pleasure! a hell upon earth if one were to dive into the abyss of Chinese life! Dust, dirt and destruction. It is impossible for any civilised being to imagine what Peking is, and the next winter will be a fearful one for the inhabitants.

The Emperor of China is never likely to leave his dominions [this in answer to a question]. The three things required of the Chinese are the establishment of Railways and Telegraphs, audience with the Emperor, and Embassies. If all the foreign representatives cooperated for these objects, they might be effected but the jealousies are too great. England and America would go hand in hand, and perhaps Prussia might join them. But France would want their Jesuits in the Interior, and Russia does not seek the advancement of China. Altogether things are in a great muddle here, and Hart has a hard time of it, having to keep in with the foreigners and the Chinese.

8 December 1867 [Mr Burlingame, the American minister, was starting on his tour of all the European courts to plead the case for China]. Mr Burlingame was detained halfway between this [city] and Tientsin, on account of rebels infesting the roads, but I believe it was all fear and suspicion. There are no doubt thieves and robbers but no rebels in our neighbourhood. At any rate there is a gunboat stationed at Tientsin for the winter, and some of the Legation escort started from this [city] for his relief, and were met by a dozen or so of Bluejackets, who escorted Mr and Mrs Burlingame and suite to Tientsin. Mr Brown, with the Chinese, leaves in a fortnight or so overland—they will number over 50, and will have a guard of mounted Chinese.

I dined last night at the British Legation (Lady Alcock's). I wish I could refuse all these invitations, as it is a punishment to go out these cold nights in a cart.

24 Dec. 1867 [He was proud of the mess, of which he was secretary, and it is obvious that they did themselves pretty well]. Our dinners are now being spoken of as the best in Peking. Tomorrow, Xmas Day, we all dine en famille. We shall have real Turtle Soup and a mayonnaise of salmon (iced punch after the soup and Sauterne after the salmon), Patés Russes, a ragout of venison, and a galantine of some kind, Roast beef and boiled turkey, Asparagus, Pheasants and salad, plum pudding, mince pies etc.

9 April 1868 [after his return from Japan]. I could not help chuck-ling at the blissful ignorance that caused you all to upbraid me for not studying Chinese on my trip to Japan. But I had other things to think of. On the river from Peking to Tientsin I enjoyed my deliverance from everyday office work. From Tientsin to Shanghai, a voyage of 5 days only (12 hours or so being spent at Chefoo), I had to make an official report on various matters. Arrived at Shanghai, I proceeded to Ningpo to report on affairs there. At Shanghai, besides the special duty upon which I was sent, I had other official work to attend to . . . I was de-lighted with my voyage to Yokohama, and my eyes were always direc-ted to the caleidoscopic scenery of the Inland Sea. At Yokohama busi-ness occupied my thoughts, and the spare time I had was devoted to exploring the neighbourhood. From Yokohama to Shanghai I was sea-bewildered, for the passage was a rough one, and so was the passage from Shanghai to Tientsin, and from Tientsin to Peking I did the jour-ney by cart, travelling all night. The idea of studying Chinese under such conditions is preposterous and ridiculous!

30 April 1868. We have had cricket in the Temple of Heaven!! and we actually managed to get 2 elevens—Irish and Scotch v. Welsh and English. I was Captain of the former and seeing that I had not played since 1862, and that I have a broken leg, I managed better than I expec-ted. I kept the wicket and caught two and stumped two . . . It is re-ported that the rebels are close to Tientsin, and that the inhabitants are in fear and trembling. No one seems to fear them here—the Chinese say "no can," "no dare"—Anglice, they cannot and dare not come. Much

will depend on the young Emperor when he comes of age. The fate of the present dynasty and the Empire will depend upon him.

14 May 1868 [mostly in praise of Hart]. The rebels have disappeared from before Tientsin to turn up somewhere else. It strikes me that they and the Imperialists are one in body and understanding; certainly the one are as bad as the other, and they slaughter right and left. The newspapers have been attacking Hart's policy in very violent language, but they know not what they say. They are endeavouring to sting him into answering; but he very wisely abstains from print and from newspaper controversy. There will be all the greater reaction by and by in his favour. He is working away quietly and silently, and his work will show itself in time. He is preparing the ground for seed, which has to be sown before the crops. He has just been organising a Marine Department in connection with the Customs, and by these and other means, in the course of perhaps some 18 months, the coast of China will be lighted where lights are most required; there will be an efficient Pilotage, a coastguard etc.

Campbell's second stay in Peking was again to be short, for in July 1868 he was sent by the Tsungli Yamen on a special mission to Europe with the rank of commissioner. Arriving at Marseilles on 19 September, exactly two years after he and Hart had last sailed for China, he was greeted with the melancholy news of his only sister's tragic death from accidental poisoning. What exactly the mission was with which he had been entrusted the papers do not show, but he was in Europe for nearly a year, and his business took him to London, Paris, Lisbon, Madrid, and Germany.

At the end of August 1869 he again left for China. His mother seems to have felt that she would never see him again. She wrote in her diary: "30 Aug. 1869. It was a grievous parting. God knows whether we shall ever meet again on earth but I fervently pray that we may all meet again in heaven. May God protect and guide him through this vale of sorrows, at the best it is nothing else. Dear Robert has gone with him as far as Paris." He reached Peking at the end of October 1869 and almost at once proceeded round the treaty ports with Hart. On 18 November he wrote from Peking: "I am pretty comfortable in my house which is to be warmed tonight by a dinner party consisting of Captain Forbes, Mr Brown, young Mr Hart, Mr Wirters (late acting Chief Secretary), Mr O'Brien (one of the Professors at the College), and Mr Baber (at the British legation)." Campbell had been entrusted by Hart with the preparation of a system of accounts for the Customs, a work for which his previous experience in the Treasury peculiarly fitted him, and his system was now to be adopted at all the ports. The intention had been that he and Hart should visit all the ports in turn in order to set the new system into operation, but before the tour could be completed the quarrel between Hart and von Gumpach came to a head, and Campbell had to be despatched to Shanghai to watch over the proceedings in Britain's consular court there. It was while he was in Shanghai in April 1870 that he heard of his mother's death; she had died at Clifton in February, her last thought being of her beloved son and the last entry in her diary relating to him. In a very feeble hand she wrote: "9 Feb. 1870—Darling Jimmie's birthday. I tried to write him a few lines by the mail. His father and sister [*sic*, though she was dead] are also writing to him." I find a sorrowful letter from him to his father dated Shanghai, 13 April 1870, in which he deplores his misfortune in being absent when first his sister and then his mother died. Hart, ever sympathetic to those in trouble, at once gave him six months' leave of absence on half pay, and he returned to England, never again, as it turned out, to come back to China.

It was while he was away on leave that he married in Brighton, on 22 September 1870, my mother Ellen Mary Lewis, "a wonderful wife of beauty, talent and charm," as Paul King described her.*

*King, p. 298.

IV

THE LONDON OFFICE OF THE CHINESE CUSTOMS SERVICE

Towards the end of 1870 Hart took advantage of Campbell's presence in Europe on leave to entrust to him the responsibility for the von Gumpach case, which was then on appeal to the Privy Council in London. Hart, when in Europe in 1866, had rather rashly, and contrary to Campbell's advice, appointed von Gumpach as professor of mathematics and astronomy at the new college in Peking for the teaching of Western languages and sciences which had recently been authorized by the Chinese government. Von Gumpach had been troublesome from the first, and when at last given his *congé* by Hart he brought action against him for wrongful dismissal. The action was tried in the consular court at Shanghai and was there decided in von Gumpach's favour, with large damages. Hart at once appealed, his chief object being to establish the point that the I. G. of Chinese Customs, although a British subject, was not amenable to British courts for lawful acts done by him as an official serving the Chinese government. The English counsel selected for Hart was Sir Roundell Palmer, K. C., who subsequently became Lord Chancellor Selborne. He seems to have been chosen because of his known sympathies with China. He had been one of a number of M. P.'s, included amongst them Gladstone and Disraeli (both curiously united on this occasion), who had protested vigorously in 1857 against the action of Lord Palmerston's government in going to war with China because of an alleged affront to the British flag when it was flying (wrongfully, as was subsequently shown) over the *Arrow*, a Chinese lorcha.

Hart's appeal seems to have been entirely successful, and on its conclusion the intention was that Campbell should return to China in order to set into operation the system of accounts which had been authorised before he left China. The chief revenue cruiser, the *Peng-chou-hoi*, had been placed under his orders and was to take him to all the southern as well as the three northern ports. Hart, however, had found Campbell's services in the numerous European transactions in which he had begun to employ him so useful that he suddenly began to think seriously of employing him permanently in Europe as "non-resident secretary," a curious title invented by himself and

intended to mean secretary non-resident in Peking. A long correspondence
ensued between the two, and I give some extracts from Hart's letters:

14 March 1873. I was just thinking this morning that, if I could get
someone who would suit me in the position of Chief Sec. as well as you
do, you would make a capital agent in Europe; or to put it another way,
what a catch it would be, if I could get someone like you for general
work in Europe!

29 May 1873. I should much rather have *you* here than anyone else;
but should you not be able to come [he wrote this because Campbell
had been ill] I should rather have *you* in London than any other person . . .

31 Aug. 1873. The question now is, are you to stay at home or are
you to come out in spring? First of all, remember this: I know of no
one who would suit me here as Chief Sec. as well as yourself—I would
rather have you than anyone I know of. If you don't come, I shall suf-
fer various kinds of inconvenience for some year or two more: (your
absence during the last two years has been an immense nuisance—I would
rather have paid von G. his £1800 down and had you at your proper
work!) Against my desire to have you here and your fitness for the post
in Peking, I must remember that, from the way you have acted during
the last two years at home, it is evident you would, in other important
ways, be as useful to me at home as you could be here: and no strange
man at home could be as useful to me as a man who knows China (as
you do), and no one could be fully employed and usefully employed
except a man thoroughly trusted by me (as you are) and personally
loyal to me (as I fully believe you to be).

The result of all this correspondence was that at the end of 1873
Campbell—somewhat to his reluctance, for he had been anxious to return
to China—was definitely appointed to organise and take charge of the
London office of the Customs, London being chosen as the commercial
centre of Europe. Mr H. C. Batchelor, who had hitherto acted as purchasing
and forwarding agent for the Chinese Customs in a half-time capacity, was
at the same time relieved of his post. Campbell never went back to China,
though, as we shall see, he was near to doing so at the time of the Boxer Rising.
From 1873 onwards till his death in 1907 he acted as Hart's alter ego in
London and Europe. His property in Peking was sold; though much of it

was lost, it fetched a considerable sum, his piano going to the Russian ambassador, and his wine, of which he had laid in a good store—evidence of his good living when in Peking—being eagerly bought up.

The premises chosen for the new office were 8 Storey's Gate, an old rambling building, now long since pulled down, which commanded a delightful view over Saint James's Park— a *rus in urbe* Campbell called it. The lease came to an end in 1892 and the office was then moved to 26 Old Queen Street, where it has been housed ever since, though it no longer occupies the whole house.

The London office came in time to be regarded as the jewel of the Service, and posts in it were eagerly sought after. Its work, however, was a bit of a mystery to the outsider. It acted as a kind of stationery and supply office for the whole Service, also as an information bureau and an examination centre. That much was known of it. But a large part of its work was highly confidential, and all who joined it were under a pledge of secrecy not to divulge, under the severest penalties, what was done. It was a hush-hush office. Its work was indeed of a most varied nature, breaking out in many new places from time to time. It ranged from the mere ordering of supplies to matters sometimes of high international importance, and Campbell's duties took him on occasion to nearly all the European capitals—to Paris, Vienna, Berne, Rome, Madrid, Lisbon (but never, so far as I can find, to Berlin, which is curious). An account of some of the work done by the London office is given in the following pages.

Campbell, as head of the London office, was mainly responsible for the creation of the at one time powerful Chinese fleet; he negotiated in Paris, on behalf of China, a treaty of peace between France and China and in Lisbon a commercial treaty between Portugal and China; he organised China's magnificent contributions to the great South Kensington exhibitions of the eighties; he was placed in charge of the special envoys sent by China to Queen Victoria's Diamond Jubilee and to King Edward VII's coronation; he took a prominent part in the organisation of China's lighthouse and postal service, and so on. The truth of the matter is that during the last three decades of the nineteenth century, when Hart was in his prime, the Customs administration under that great man was so highly valued by the Chinese government that all sorts of new activities were entrusted to it, and as Hart's sphere of operations extended so did that of his alter ego in London.

In addition to all this, questions of international law frequently arose and these were all dealt with by the London office in consultation with the famous old firm of Murray, Hutchins, and Sterling of Birchin Lane. I remember that when an especially difficult legal problem occurred, Campbell and Mr Hutchins, the head of the firm, would often go off together to stay for a few days at the Granville Hotel in Ramsgate, where, in the large room placed at their disposal, they could concentrate uninterruptedly on their task, in the good sea air. The London office did things in the grand style in those days.

Campbell's long experience in the Home Civil Service and his intimacy with the heads of the chief government departments rendered him an ideal head for the new office, and the way in which he organised the work and arranged for such matters as the registration and filing of papers and the keeping of accounts won general admiration from those who were privileged to serve under him. Needless to say, his accounts were a model of simplicity and exactness. Paul King in his book mentions his "wonderful knowledge of official account keeping," and so great a reputation did he acquire for accountancy that he was asked towards the end of his life to write a book on the subject; unfortunately he did not live to complete it. It was no doubt the sound training he had received at the Treasury and the Audit Office that had inspired Lay, and Hart after him, to appoint him as audit secretary of the Customs.

The system of accounts that he drafted for the Service before leaving China in 1870, with a few alterations subsequently made by him to meet changing conditions, stood the test of time. On his appointment as head of the London office, the post of auditor in China was filled by others, but Campbell was still the recognised authority on accounts and no alteration in the system was made without consulting him; indeed in 1878 there was some talk of his going out to China, *en mission extraordinaire*, to look into the working of the system. In this, one of his pet subjects, Campbell did not readily brook interference, and when a clever junior in the Service once ventured to criticize the system in a long memorandum, which Hart sent on to Campbell for his observations, Campbell indulged in a crushing reply. Finlay Smith, an expert mathematician, was auditor at the time, and Campbell took advantage of his presence in London on leave to show him his reply before he sent it. The latter wrote, "I am very pleased with the Memo. I am glad you have gone into the question at such length, and especially glad am I that you uphold the present system throughout with such firmness. The whole thing too in such quiet and temperate language that you cannot possibly be charged with displaying feeling." Hart, who was probably secretly amused at Campbell's outburst, wrote to him, "What a man you are to take a steam-hammer to crush a mosquito!" Years later Finlay Smith wrote from Peking, "I do not think we need fear any change in our sound system of accounting—the system is too good to be easily overthrown."

When to all this is added the superior despatch style and the very considerable diplomatic talents that King ascribes to Campbell, it is no wonder that a training under him was eagerly sought by those who aspired to climb high in the Service, as many who served under him subsequently did; to mention only a few names, there were H. M. Hillier, Alfred E. Hippisley, Hosea B. Morse, F. E. Taylor, and his own cousin Smollett Campbell.

Campbell demanded and obtained a high standard of work from his staff, but out of office hours he was kind and considerate, constantly entertaining his colleagues to dinner at his home. Often I used to hear him say to my mother, "Mr____has not dined here for some time; you had better ask him." Also every New Year he gave an elaborate dinner to which were invited not only his own staff but all members of the Service who happened to be home on leave, as well as the Chinese minister in London and members of the legation staff. These annual New Year dinners became quite famous in the Service.

Campbell certainly set an example of hard work himself. His normal working day at the office was from 10:30 to 7:00. Punctually every morning at ten his carriage fetched him, and sharp at a quarter to seven it called at the office to take him home, always stopping at the Thatched House Club, where he would get out to have a glass of sherry and buy a cigar to smoke en route. He scarcely ever took a holiday, his only relaxation being an afternoon occasionally during the summer at his beloved oval to watch Surrey at cricket and a week perhaps at Brighton to attend the Sussex cricket week. As Paul King remarks, "If he had a small endearing weakness it was a love for first-class cricket that was more than a love—a relic no doubt from his Cheltenham days. Stolen fruit in his case, for his rule was to devote every hour of the day and much of each night to his official duties. Still if an unusually long absence from the Office occurred sometimes in the Cricket season no one ever had the bad taste to inquire who won the match!"*

So wedded to the office did he become that whenever his family was away on holiday he took up his quarters there, sleeping in a room which he had furnished himself. He even went to the office on Sundays. On that day he usually attended to Hart's private affairs (he was trustee under Hart's marriage settlement), and he liked to have one day free from all interference. Sunday was also the day which he set apart for correspondence with his numerous Service friends. As time went on he came to be regarded as the Nestor of the Service, and his advice on all sorts of matters was freely sought and as freely given. He kept copies of most of his letters and I have been through some hundreds of them. He could be all things to all men. Advice, encouragement, consultation, and rebuke are all to be found, as well as shrewd comments on the political events of the time. He used often, too, to have his jokes, particularly with the gay and genial James Hart, brother of the I. G. Here are a few extracts taken at random:

29 Oct. 1875 [to a newly wedded commissioner]. Hannen has ordered your furniture . . . There is no greater mistake in housekeeping than to purchase cheap furniture.

30 Nov. 1877 [to an irrate commissioner]. You must have patience, a virtue which I have to exercise here to an extraordinary degree.

19 July 1878 [to a commissioner in trouble]. What a grand thing it would be if one could pass through life without troubles of any kind, but they always crop up when least expected.

1 Dec. 1878 [to a commissioner who is fond of good wine]. You ought to let me send you out some really good claret and Burgundy . . . I have laid in a stock of wine myself which I chose at the Café Voisin . . . I am sure that nothing does a man so much harm as drinking the wines that are sold in the East. If I were you I should order out a supply of

*King, p. 298.

wine for 2 years (or even for 3) and then indent annually for the quantity you require to make up your 2 years stock . . . This is the principle on which all supplies should be ordered for the Service—especially Light House Stores etc. One of these days you will run short of wicks or mineral oil—the Suez Canal will be blocked or blockaded—and your Lights will be put out!

1 Dec. 1878 [to a confirmed bachelor commissioner]. I am glad you like N'Chwang; but, my dear fellow, you ought to have a wife there—it is the very place where a person can live on love and matrimony.

20 Dec. 1878 [to the commissioner above who is fond of his wine]. I am sorry to hear that your liver cannot stand a glass of two of champagne: "Quantum mutatus ab illo." You must exercise self denial, and save yourself for your next visit to Europe.

2 Sept. 1887 [to a commissioner who is alarmed at his growing corpulence]. I have been making inquiries concerning Mr. Russell's treatment for corpulence. I hear it is one of those quack medicines which impose upon the crowd and that there is nothing in it . . . You can however try the effect of a simple remedy which will not cost you anything, viz., to drink before breakfast and dinner a pint of hot water; eat no bread; and do not eat any fat with your meat or indulge in butter or oil; avoid wine and restrict yourself to 2 glasses of beer a day. Such I am told is the present treatment recommended in the Medical Journals.

26 August 1892 [to a commissioner who seeks advice about investments]. If you still desire to invest money otherwise than in the English Funds, you can telegraph to me the word "Spread"; and I will only invest in the Securities named by yourself. But, if you will take my advice you will leave matters as they are. You will feel more comfortable and so shall I. I take better care of my neighbour's horse than I do of my own—and I preach better than I practice . . . The only safe advice I give is: "put your money in the funds," and you can then sleep without anxiety!

5 April 1889 [to James Hart, who is discouraged about his Sikkim-Tibet negotiations]. It is just when a negotiation appears to be in articulo mortis that a change for the better takes place, and I trust it will be in your case.

8 Jan. 1875 [rebuke to an assistant commissioner]. I am glad that
you have given up connection with the Chinese girl . . . I must say that
I think ____ acted very kindly and considerately in warning you of the
evil consequences that would result from your living maritalement with
a Chinese woman. He might have put before you his own experience as
a caution. Remember that "qui s'excuse s'accuse" and that the "tu
quoque" or "ad hominem" argument is the poorest logic and the most
puerile defence. Verbum sap!

7 Nov. 1876 [rebuke to a commissioner who has failed to keep his
promise]. When a friend undertakes a service for another, it becomes
a duty upon him to fulfil it.

17 March 1894 [rebuke to ____ about failure to send receipts]. A
missing receipt renders the record of proceedings, in connection with
an order, incomplete, and the want of it has been frequently felt. When
the receipt is not forthcoming in due course, we are apprehensive that
something may be wrong; and, as you can well understand, it is a great
satisfaction to know that all is right.

26 June 1896 [to Paul King, who has left the London office for China,
a letter of appreciation]. The Office seems very strange and dull without
you . . . I shall always look back with much pleasure upon the time you
have served in this Office—feeling personally grateful to you for the assistance you have always so readily, cheerfully and effectively given.

Of much greater interest to the historian, however, are the references
in these occasional letters to his friends to current political events. During
Campbell's long reign at the London office both China and Europe passed
through many serious crises, and I give in Appendix 1 some of Campbell's
comments on these events written in Stoic calm from his office chair. I also
give in Appendix 2 extracts (mainly political) from letters written to Campbell from his China friends. The two appendices taken together give a kind
of running commentary on the chief political events of the period.**

Friday evening at the office was always rather hectic. Friday, known as
mail day, was the day the weekly mail was sent to Hart. During all the time

**References to materials intended for the missing appendices are marked with a double asterisk
throughout. See Foreword.

that Hart was in Peking and Campbell in London, weekly letters passed between the two, Campbell including in his letter a review of political events in Europe, with any bearing they might have on China, while Hart reviewed China events from his end. These letters certainly yield an interesting picture of Chinese and European history from 1874 to 1907. Campbell began writing his mail letter about five o'clock, and from that moment onwards his room was sacrosanct; woe betide anyone who had the temerity to interrupt. Exactly at a quarter to seven the bell would ring for his most efficient office-manager, Henry Sinstadt, whose function on these occasions was to make a copy of the letter in the letter press and, that done, to stand by with candle burning to light the sealing wax, on which Campbell would then impress the Craignish seal.

I have mentioned the efficient Sinstadt, but no account of the London office would be complete without some reference to its coachman James Botting, who spent a lifetime in the Customs Service and was a really striking character. It should be mentioned that Campbell received, in addition to his pay, a special allowance which enabled him to keep coachman, horse, carriage, and stables. Campbell's business took him frequently to the City, where he paid visits with an almost routine regularity to the Customs' solicitors, Murray, Hutchins, and Sterling; to the old firm of Tallack in Great Saint Helens, who had from the first managed in the most efficient manner the whole of the vast amount of shipping needed to meet the Customs requirements; to the manager of the Hongkong and Shanghai Bank, to stockbroker Panmure Gordon, and to other City magnates concerned with China's financial affairs. And here let me say how greatly missed by the City Campbell was when he died. His reputation as an expert on China finance lived on, and many years after his death I was told by the chairman of the British and Chinese Corporation that since his departure things in the City had never been the same so far as China was concerned, and that there were still many of them left who sighed for the good old days of Hart and Campbell.

But to return to James Botting. The ways of his master were so well known to him that it was seldom necessary for any directions to be given, and hardly a word passed between the two. "The City" was all his master said as he entered his carriage, and to the City Botting went, stopping at place after place without a word said. Then, all done, at the single word

"Home" off Botting went, being careful, however, always to stop a few moments at Birch's, where Campbell got out to have a glass of sherry. During his long wait for his master Botting was often to be seen with a broad grin on his rubicund face. He was gifted with a talent for making jokes which he often sent to the comic papers, making quite a decent sum of money in this way. A grin on his face meant that another joke had been hatched, and the policeman passing by (he was known to all the City police) would exclaim, "Well, James, what's the latest?" Faithful James Botting; on his master's death his services were no longer required and he retired to Broadstairs where he was well looked after by our family.

It seems fitting to say a few words here about the Chinese Legation and its relations with the London office. People have often wondered how it was that, during the Hart-Campbell regime, the London office, besides engaging in its own distinctive activities, was sometimes entrusted by the Chinese government with matters which ordinarily would have been managed by China's own diplomatic representative in London. It is rather curious, for example, to find that the legation took no part in the international exhibitions of 1883, 1884, and 1885, which were arranged by Campbell and Hart alone; that it was to Hart and Campbell that the Chinese government entrusted the negotiation of such important treaties as those with France in 1885 and with Portugal in 1887; that it was Campbell again who was charged with the responsibility of looking after the Chinese special envoys who attended Queen Victoria's Diamond Jubilee of 1897 and King Edward's coronation in 1902. It is significant too that the legation took no part in the Sikkim-Tibet Convention and subsequent trade regulations, which were negotiated by Hart directly from Peking between 1889 and 1893. The explanation is probably to be found in the fact that the Chinese Legation was then in its infancy—it had only started in 1877—and during these early years, while the minister and his staff were learning their work, the Chinese government looked to the experienced head of the London office for the negotiation of many important matters.

It was indeed late in the day before China decided to have her own diplomatic representatives abroad, and it was not until 1875-1876 that she constituted her first two missions—one for England, the other for the United States, Spain, and Peru. The London office had already been four years in existence when China's first minister to the Court of Saint James took up his residence in London in quarters engaged for him by Campbell. His name was Kuo Sung-tao, and he was accompanied by Dr Macartney (afterwards Sir Halliday Macartney) as chief of staff. According to some interesting letters written at the time by Mr William Cartwright,** Chinese secretary in the Customs, who had himself been approached about becoming secretary to the legation, there seems to have been some difficulty in Peking over both appointments. There were plenty of men only too eager for the subordinate posts, but there was not the same enthusiasm for the higher. Kuo had at first declined the appointment and had gone for some time into obstinate retirement, while more than one Customs commissioner, in addition to Cartwright, had refused the post of secretary. Dr Macartney was not himself a Customs man and there was some disappointment in the Service that one of its members had not been finally chosen. The British legation in Peking were secretly pleased, however, according to Cartwright, for they were becoming jealous of Hart's growing power and regarded the appointment of a non-Customs man as a check to his political ambition.

Kuo arrived in London in January 1877 and lost no time in seeking Campbell's assistance and advice. Almost his first act was to call upon him after dinner one evening at his home in Clanricarde Gardens, where he stayed talking till midnight. Campbell found the task of initiating the minister into his new duties rather difficult, because he had received no official instructions as to what his relations with him were to be. However, he had infinite tact and common sense and the two speedily became friends. Kuo made a point of attending Campbell's New Year dinner, and various civilities passed between their respective wives. A son was born to the minister in March 1878 and my mother was amused though pleased when the minister's wife acknowledged her inquiries by sending her a present of twenty red eggs! Kuo's stay in London was of short duration; shortly after the opening of the Paris Exhibition of 1878 he left for Paris.

Kuo was succeeded by Marquis Tseng (Tseng Chi-tse), an ambitious man who sought to gain distinction in the diplomatic field. He spent a large part of 1880 in Saint Petersburg, where he was successful in arranging a treaty between Russia and China on the Ili frontier question, but when later he tried to settle in Paris the quarrel between France and China over Tongking he failed and, becoming *persona non grata* with the French, had to leave Paris in chagrin. There were some, however, who attributed that failure to Macartney rather than to the marquis himself. It was after this that Hart and Campbell stepped in and, as we shall see, achieved a wonderful success. In London the marquis made himself very popular, and when he returned to China in 1886 with seven years' experience gained in Europe, great things were expected of him. Indeed in 1888, when Hart was contemplating resignation, there was some talk of his succeeding him as Inspector General. But Hart did not resign, and in any case, as Cartwright wrote in one of his letters, there was one man who would have opposed his appointment and whose opposition would have been fatal—Li Hung-chang, whom he had greatly annoyed by his Paris negotiations in 1884. Instead the marquis was made partly responsible, with Prince Ch'un, for naval affairs. Although the marquis, by his strong backing of the Chinese war party, had perhaps unknowingly impeded Campbell's work during the last stages of the Paris peace negotiations of 1885, Campbell bore him no ill feeling. His relations with him continued to be friendly and cordial and the two kept up their friendship by corresponding long after the marquis had left. I still have photographs of the marquis, his wife, and their little son.

The ministers who followed were: 1886-1890, Liu Jui-fen; 1890-1894, Hsüeh Fu-ch'eng; 1894-1897, Kung Chao-yüan; 1897-1902, Lo Feng-luh; 1902-1905, Chang Te-i; 1906-1907, Wang Ta-hsieh; 1907-1910, Lord Li Ching-fang. Campbell's relations with them all continued to be of the friendliest character, and for Lo Feng-luh in particular he had a warm regard. The latter, who was a friend of the great Li Hung-chang, had particularly wanted to act as secretary to the Chinese special envoy at Queen Victoria's Diamond Jubilee, and Campbell was not a little gratified when Lo consented gracefully to retire on hearing that it was the emperor's desire that Campbell, and not he, should act in that capacity. He and Campbell saw a great deal of one another during the anxious days of the Boxer Rising and were almost alone in combating the prevalent view that all the foreigners in Peking had been massacred.

As already intimated, the early Chinese ministers seldom took any important step without consulting Campbell, and the British Foreign Office likewise frequently consulted him. But as time went on and the Chinese

Legation became more experienced, it became less necessary for the London office to intervene, and things were greatly altered after the reform edicts of 1906, which, in the opinion of many, though perhaps not of Hart himself, definitely lowered the status of the Customs Service. In his last letters to Campbell Hart rather pathetically tried to make out that his own position had not been affected, and that he was as much trusted by the Chinese as ever. Be that as it may, when both he and Campbell finally passed away, the days when the Service had been entrusted with important diplomatic work were gone forever; henceforward the Chinese Legation reigned supreme in its own province. It is pleasing to know, however, that even to this day (I am writing in 1944) the relations between London office and legation continue to be of a cordial nature.

I shall now proceed to give a more detailed account of some of the work done by the London office, beginning with the entrance examination to the Service, which from the first was placed under Campbell's charge.

V

THE SERVICE'S ENTRANCE EXAMINATION

During the greater part of Sir Robert Hart's reign there was keen competition for entry into the Chinese Imperial Maritime Customs Service, an appointment in the Service being regarded, by those who knew, as almost if not quite as good as an appointment in our own Indian Civil Service. The name chosen for the Service (apart from the one dignified word "imperial") was perhaps a little unfortunate and rather conveyed the impression that its work must be similar to that of the *douanes* of European countries, which were then, as now, generally regarded as the lowest in rank of government departments. This, of course, was far from being the case; the holder of a post in the Chinese Customs Service at once attained a high social status in the East, whilst one fortunate enough to become a "commissioner of customs" (another unhappy title) was a very important person indeed. Moreover, from a pecuniary point of view the Service was attractive enough. The lowest administrative officer (4th assistant B) began with a salary of £400 a year (as compared with £250 in a home government department), received a handsome travelling and equipment allowance, and at the end of every seven years was entitled to two years' leave on half pay, plus an extra year's pay (which he was expected to treat as capital in lieu of a retiring allowance).

In the early days, it is true, there was some doubt as to whether the Service would last, but as time went on and the benefits derived from its sound honest administration were gradually recognised both by China herself and the powers generally, its permanence, barring any world catastrophe, seemed assured. Hart had made a report on the Service to the British government in 1865; and in 1879, on the eve of his return to China after a few months' leave in Europe (the last leave he allowed himself before his final departure from China in 1908, by the way), he was asked to reply to certain questions put to him by a member of Parliament. The questions and the replies are so interesting that I give them in full:

Q. The relations between the Local Authorities and the Commissioners of Customs at each port. How far are the latter under the order or control of the former in ther performance of their duties?

A. They are Colleagues. The Commissioner is not the Superintendent's Subordinate. If the two differ in opinion, the opinion of the Supt, as being the native official, is to prevail pending reference to Peking.

Q. In cases of litigation between the merchants and Customs House are the Commissioners or their subordinates individually responsible to the Courts; or is the action against the Chinese Officials or the Government?

A. For acts done by the Commissioner as Commissioner, the Chinese Government answers.

Q. Is there in print the conditions of service for the personnel—that is, the several members or grades of the Imperial Customs? Are they liable to be dismissed at the pleasure of the Inspector General?

A. Yes; in the I.G.'s Circulars, not published for the Public. Yes; but such an exercise of authority is of very rare occurrence.

Q. Many important and subsidiary services have been organised by the Inspector General—Schools, Colleges, Lights, Beacons, Pilots, Harbour Masters etc. Is there any detail of these in print?

A. Yes; there are the I.G.'s Circulars, Rules and Regulations.

Q. Do any portion of the proceeds of the customs levied at each port go to meet the expenses of the Province or Local Administration not connected with the Customs?

A. The support of the Service is the first charge. One tenth of the remainder is set apart for the support of Legations. Four tenths of the balance is devoted to coast defence. The balance goes to the General Provincial Fund.

Q. Do you think the Foreign Protectorate has now struck such deep roots in the soil that the Chinese Government would not under any circumstances revert or desire to revert to the old practice? Supposing, for instance, they were deprived, as sooner or later they must be, of its present head, would there not be great difficulties in the appointment of a successor with the jangle of Foreign Legations advocating their own nationals as candidates?

A. Earthquakes bury cities and tornadoes uproot trees. There are many reasons for hoping that the Service will be a lasting one; but the element of uncertainty about which Sir Rutherford Alcock used to talk in 1859 is still to the front even in 1879. That the Service has lived against all opposition 20 years is something in favour of its continued existence.

That Hart's optimism was justified is shown by the fact that, whereas in 1879 there were 500 Europeans and 2000 Chinese on the Customs staff, by 1897 the numbers had increased to 700 and 4000 respectively, and later there was a still further increase. Even in 1907, when the Chinese were beginning to assume greater control over their own affairs and Hart himself was beginning to appoint Chinese to posts of greater responsibility, he anticipated profitable activity by the Service. "The Service has still some decades before it, and my successor will find the post and position very big indeed, and, if well handled will make much out of both," he wrote to me just before leaving China after Campbell's death.

Nominations rested with Hart himself. The numerous applications for an appointment which Campbell received were always sent by him to Peking, with a photograph of the applicant, and he made it a rule never to recommend anyone for nomination himself. The duty of passing or rejecting candidates rested with him and he felt that he must be above suspicion. Both Hart and Campbell were frequently approached with requests for nominations from the most exalted quarters in England and elsewhere. I have found letters addressed to my father from, for example, Jules Ferry, Sir Julian Pauncefote, Prince Rospigliosi, and many other celebrities, and on one occasion the great General Charles Gordon, who rarely sought favours, wrote from Jerusalem to advance the claims of a young friend. Gordon, by the way, was a close friend of Campbell's and godfather to his youngest son. Not infrequently, however, the reply to these applications had to be "No vacancies" or "No British vacancies."

The one black spot in the Service was that all members of the staff were at the mercy of one man, liable to transfer or dismissal at his pleasure. On the whole, however, dismissals were rare, and Hart was a benevolent despot who did many little acts of kindness of which the world knew nothing (especially on his birthday, which was a favourite day with him for making his promotions). He had his enemies, of course, who accused him of favouritism in his promotions, and there is no doubt but that he did favour his own and his wife's relations. He liked to consider himself impartial, however, and I have come across the following memorandum written by him in response to a request by a certain exalted personage that a protégé of his be promoted:

33

Sir Robert Hart had the honour to meet the Duke of __ and suite
at Peking, and on the application of __ gave a nomination to his son.
The son, M.__joined the Service in 1872 and received his earlier promotions somewhat rapidly in recognition of some work he had done
of a scientific kind; it is now some time since he was last promoted, and
he is now being judged by his official qualifications as an office man,
and not by his scientific tastes or abilities. He has the character of being
a man of high principles and his conduct is all that could be desired, but,
in the office, his work is, in respect of quality, below the average.

In the Customs Service it is not interest that secures men their promotion; it is work. The man who does not work satisfactorily is advanced
slowly or not at all, no matter who his friends are; while the man who
works well makes his way rapidly to the front without recommenda-
tions from outside—and all the more rapidly if absolutely friendless.
Sir Robert Hart will have much pleasure in bearing in mind the wishes
of the high personages interested in M.__, but his own responsibilities
vis à vis the Chinese Government and the Service will not allow him to
rate M.__'s work at any time above what it is worth from a Service
point of view.

This was written in Peking on 31 August 1883. Admirable, had the principles
always been followed!

And now a few words about the examination itself. Hart, naturally, kept
some general control. He settled, for example, the minimum standard of at-
tainment to be expected, and the age limits (nineteen to twenty-three, with
a preference for those who were nearer twenty-three than nineteen), but the
actual details and conduct of the examination he left entirely to Campbell,
his only stipulation being that the papers of all successful candidates should
be sent to him in Peking so that he might be able to form some preliminary
judgment of their capabilities. This was but one instance of the way in which
the great man kept an eye on his junior staff members, who found out, sometimes to their cost, that there was little he did not know about them. Hart
also gave to Campbell a rather unusual discretionary power, which would
probably have startled the ordinary professional examiner of those days. "If,"
he wrote in a private letter to Campbell, "after selecting 5, you still see among
the other candidates one man to whom you would like to give an appointment, you may issue a 6th, but this 6th is not a proxime accessit, but to enable
you to gratify taste of instinct, or a feeling of preference not allowable to an

Examiner." I do not know whether Campbell ever exercised this power, but I have come across one case in which he deliberately refused to use it, even though he was rather persistently asked to do so by no less a person than Lady Hart herself in favour of one of her young friends.

Every year, and sometimes oftener, a batch of candidates came to the London office for examination. Examination was merely qualifying for a favoured few, such as sons of commissioners, but generally it was both qualifying and then competitive for those who had passed the qualifying test. No one was excused the qualifying examination, and Campbell occasionally got a scare when, as sometimes happened, a more than usually brilliant candidate only just managed to scrape through the arithmetic, although at this stage of the examination it did not go beyond vulgar and decimal fractions. Thus I find him writing to the commissioner brother of a university candidate, "You would be surprised to hear how rusty your brother had become in Arithmetic and Addition; he was first, however, in the competitive examination *albis equis*, which I believe is the Latin for Long Chalks." Unfortunately for the Service, this particular candidate never took up his appointment but became instead one of Her Majesty's inspectors of schools!

Great preparations for the examination were made at the London office beforehand. Everything was made as comfortable as possible for the candidates, and Campbell made it his regular practice during the examination to take each of them in turn to lunch at the Thatched House Club in Saint James's Street, partly out of kindness, partly in order to study their appearance and manners and to judge their general suitability for a Service in which infinite tact and common sense were required. His general attitude may best be expressed in his own words written to one of his China friends in 1877: "I examine each man according to his own statement, to see whether his performance comes up to his professions; I look at him from all sides, educationally, physically, morally, intellectually etc., and then, out of the many candidates I select the few who are the best, taking them all round." There was, of course, a medical examination, and this was entrusted to Dr Colin MacRae, a noted Eastern doctor, who had been the close friend and medical attendant of Lord Elgin, Viceroy of India.

Hundreds of candidates passed through Campbell's hands during the thirty-four-odd years he was head of the London office, most of the English

ones coming from our public schools, and it is of interest to record his views
on their previous education, deliberately formed after this long experience.
He wrote to his friend William Cartwright in 1892, "The more I see of young
fellows coming from Public Schools, the more I am convinced that there is
nothing like a sound Classical training." Striking independent testimony this
in support of those who, in these materialistic days, still have the courage to
press for the retention of the classics in our schools as, after all, the best
general training for the mind. Campbell offered these words of advice to a
commissioner friend who was proposing to remove his boy from his public
school in order that he might specially prepare for the Customs examination:

It is very difficult to advise you as to what you should do with the
boy—whether to keep him at the College or to send him abroad, and it
is a question which I think could be best answered by Mr Baker [his
house-master]. I find that when boys leave school at an early age to
study French and German, they neglect their own language, and fail in
orthography, grammar and composition, as well as in the elementary
subjects—arithmetic, History and Geography—whilst they forget any
Latin or Greek they may have learnt. To remove a boy from a Public
School, before he has reached the highest form implies that he does
not get on, and in 99 cases out of 100 the fault of his not getting on is
attributable more to the boy himself than to his masters—because, if
other boys get on, why does not he get on?!

Having placed him at Cheltenham, I think you had better keep him
there. It is what I am doing with my own son after considering all the
pros and cons. He is one of the College Prefects, which is the highest
honour a Public School boy can attain; and it must be an excellent
training for after-life, as the Prefects have to maintain discipline, and
possess more power than the masters in the way of punishment for
offences which may not come under the Master's eyes. They must also
be on their P's and Q's and set an Example to their juniors.

I remember the infinite care which my father took in settling and correcting the examination papers, in concert with the experts who were from
time to time called in, and the delight which these occasions afforded him of
renewing his schoolboy learning. He became a boy again. He was a sound
classical scholar himself and knew his Horace, Virgil, and Ovid well. I shall
never forget one night during one of these examinations when Ralph Tanner,
second master at Westminster, came to dine at our house. Wishing to display

his classical learning, my father in high glee and to Tanner's infinite amusement rolled off quotation after quotation. Two of his favourite tags were Ovid's *Os homini sublime dedit caelumque tueri jussit*, always delivered in solemn tones, and Horace's neat compliment to a well-dressed woman, *simplex munditiis* (simple in her very neatness), this sometimes with a sly glance at his eldest daughter when her attire was more than usually elaborate. Milton and Shakespeare, too, he often quoted. "Peace hath her victories no less renowned than war," and "After life's fitful fever he sleeps well" were two favourites.

Campbell's examination work was well done and was not forgotten, for in 1924 and again in 1925, many years after his death, I was asked to take charge of a competitive examination for a large number of candidates. I had no hesitation in accepting the request and, with the help of some of my inspector colleagues at the Board of Education, appear to have managed the business satisfactorily, for I subsequently received a cordial letter of appreciation from Sir Francis Aglen, who succeeded Hart as Inspector General. It was a real pleasure to me to come into touch with the Customs Service again and to realise that my father's memory was still cherished in this indirect way.

VI

THE LIGHTING OF THE CHINESE COAST

The lighting of China's enormous coast line was not the least of the benefits which the Customs Service conferred on China. When Campbell first went out to China in 1863 there were only two or three insignificant lights in the neighbourhood of Canton, and one inferior light vessel at Shanghai. Twenty years later there were over seventy lights of a superior order, four lightships, fifty-four barges, and fifty beacons; evidence of the progress that had been made was shown in a huge map of China that covered the end wall of the Chinese Court at the Fisheries Exhibition of 1883, which marked with red discs the places on the coast where lighthouses and light-ships had been erected. A model was also exhibited of one of the most important lighthouses, that on Breaker Point in the Swatow district. It was an iron tower 120 feet in height, which had been constructed by Sir William George Armstrong's firm, and so strongly braced and supported by exterior iron rods that it had withstood the shaking of two earthquakes and the force of several typhoons. As the years went on, the lighting still further increased until finally China's dangerous coast had a lighting system, provided at great coast entirely out of Customs funds, which compared favourably with that in any other part of the world.

For this important development, which contributed materially to the interests of commerce and navigation and to the protection and advantage of China's large fishing population, Sir Robert Hart was responsible. Even if this had been his sole achievement for China it alone would have constituted a claim to greatness. The whole of the administration was left in his hands, and a special Department of Coast Lights, with its own staff of engineers, tidewaiters, and so on, was established by him for the purpose.

Campbell and his London office contributed their full share to the success. All the material came from Europe, and the ordering and supplying of all this material, as well as the selection and appointment of engineers, was one of the first tasks entrusted to Campbell. In time the work became one of the normal routine functions of the London office. Campbell was never satisfied with less than the very best, and the impartiality of the

Customs Service in its commercial dealings with foreign countries was evident. As an example, for lighting Campbell at first employed chiefly a Birmingham firm, but he discovered that France was producing a better article, and many of his later orders went to the famous Paris firm of Barbier, Benard, and Turenne. M. Barbier was a fine old Frenchman whom I remember well. The French government showed M. Barbier their appreciation for his lighthouse work by making him a Knight of the Legion of Honour.

VII

THE CHINESE FLEET AND ADMIRAL LANG

Campbell had a great deal to do with the creation of the Chinese Northern Fleet, which for a short time became the most powerful fleet in the Pacific, a fact unknown to most people. If only its administration had been kept in proper hands, how different might the history of the East have been, for a strong fleet would have enabled China to hold her own against the evil machinations of foreign powers, Russia, Japan, Germany, and the rest.

Campbell had witnessed the failure of the first gunboat fleet under Captain Sherard Osborn, and when he and Mr Lay returned with it to England in 1863 to arrange for its sale, it probably never occurred to him that he was to be instrumental in the resurrection of Chinese naval power. Yet such was to be the case, for in the summer of 1875 he received the second of his direct commissions from the Chinese government, being specially commissioned by them to purchase another gunboat fleet. China was then beginning to feel nervous about Japan's growing activities. In the previous year Japan had sent an expedition to Formosa for the purpose of obtaining satisfaction for the murder of a shipwrecked crew, and war had only been averted through the frantic efforts of the British minister, Sir Thomas Wade. But China had to pay an indemnity and felt aggrieved. And now Japan was beginning to stir up trouble in Korea. Clearly China must have a fleet.

Campbell's appointment does not seem to have been made known to the British legation in Peking until some time after the event and there was a bit of a fuss in consequence. A letter written by William Cartwright to Campbell on 21 March 1876 gave a rather amusing description of the minister's outburst:

> By this mail you will receive your appointment as the Tsung-li-Yamen's agent for the purchase of Gunboats. The British Legation made a great fuss about the insertion of the "sacred" word Consul in connection with your appointment. Wade rushed up to the Yamen and harangued them for 3 hours on the subject. "The British Treaty does not allow you to appoint a Consul in London; there is no such thing as reciprocity; a special convention must be drawn up; the appointment must be notified by Imperial Decree etc. etc." The Yamen started off a Ting Chin [*t'ing-ch'ai?*]

for the I. G., who arrived in the midst of the battle, and, after a short talk with Shen Chang Teng in the adjoining room, encountered Sir Tommy and vanquished him in 5 minutes. The Yamen despatch is to be communicated to Lord Derby and your official position will then be recognised in London.

Campbell gave his order for the building of the fleet to the firm of Sir William Armstrong of Elswick, and this was what first brought him into touch with Lord Rendel (then Mr Stuart Rendel), who was a partner in the firm. The vessels were designed by Lord Rendel's brother, Mr George Rendel, and their chief armament consisted of an enormous gun, the heaviest gun then afloat, which was carried in the bow, the idea being to attack and annihilate larger vessels at long range. The ships were named by Campbell after the Greek alphabet, the names being changed to Chinese names later, of course, and the first two of them, *Alpha* and *Beta*, set out for their long and risky voyage in the late summer of 1876. They sailed under British officers, with British crews, and under the British flag.

There was some hesitation as to which flag they should sail under. Both Hart and the Tsungli Yamen had expressed the wish that they sail under the Chinese flag, if possible, but Campbell decided otherwise. His reasons are interesting. There was at the time a possibility that war might shortly break out between Britain and China over the murder of the British consul, Mr A. R. Margary, in Yunnan in March 1875. The true story of the murder was never discovered, despite the efforts of a special joint committee of British and Chinese officials which was sent to investigate on the spot. The bare facts were these. Margary, a young and promising member of the British consular staff, had been instructed to act as interpreter to a British trade mission which was seeking to reopen trade between Burma and the southwestern provinces of China; this trade had recently been seriously interrupted by a great Mohammedan rebellion in the area. Margary had travelled the long journey from Hankow to Bhamo and had been received everywhere with the greatest courtesy and hospitality, but on the return journey, while travelling at the head of the mission, he had been treacherously murdered shortly after crossing the Chinese frontier. The British accused Chinese troops of the murder and naturally sought amends.

Tedious negotiations followed, but Sir Thomas Wade was not satisfied, despite the fact that the three officials responsible for order in the district had been handed over for trial, and there was soon a regular war scare in China. Wade made things worse in June 1876, just as matters appeared to be nearing a settlement, when he rushed off hysterically to Shanghai to communicate with his government and created the impression that war was imminent. Almost in despair, the Tsungli Yamen had to send Hart off to Shanghai to try and bring Wade to a better frame of mind. Here are some extracts from letters which Cartwright wrote to Campbell from Peking; even that able and level-headed man was clearly frightened:

6 November 1875. Merchants in China are greatly enraged at what they regard as the fruitless outcome of the negotiations. The educated classes are becoming very impatient of concessions to foreigners, and the officials who are responsible for them are becoming very unpopular. The inflammatory placards are now directed, not against us, but against them. Li Hung Chang remarked the other day to Mr Hart that he was "damned to death"—"ma sze hao wo." The I. G. remarked that his unpopularity did not seem to affect his appetite!

22 June 1876. We have been having an exciting time of it during the last fortnight. Wade has now rushed off to Shanghai to communicate with the Home Government. The Yamen is in a great state of alarm and the I. G. has been running to and fro at all hours of the day and night. The prospect looks pretty bad at present . . .

30 June 1876. We are waiting for Wade's next move. Is it to be war or peace? It looks doubtful. If Wade had not rushed off, another 24 hours negotiations would have settled matters . . .

13 July 1876. You will have heard of course of the I. G.'s departure for Shanghai. Wright and I are in charge here. Everything is quiet, but the Chinese are very apprehensive of trouble ahead. The large tablet at the tomb of the first Emperor of the present dynasty has just been split in two by lightning and this is regarded as sure omen of coming disasters . . .

Campbell, at the London end, ever serene in all China's crises, never lost confidence. It was the year of the Bulgarian atrocities and the Russian scare, and that England should go to war in the midst of these European complications seemed to him highly improbable. Out of the many letters advising calm which he wrote at this time to his anxious China friends I shall quote from only one: "You seem all of you in China to be in a terrible funk about war. Why is it that only in your China newspapers appear all these war rumours and preparations etc! . . . Do you think for one moment that the English Government would dare to attack China on account of the Yunnan business whilst defending Turkey in the face of the Bulgarian Atrocities!" Fortunately, Campbell turned out to be right. There was no war; instead we got the Chefoo Convention, with its opening of more new ports.

All the same Campbell had to guard against the possibility of war. As the trusted agent of the Chinese government, he argued that in the event of war the vessels, if sailing under the Chinese flag, would at once be seized and confiscated, whereas, if they continued to be held by him as the registered owner, they could be handed over to and become the property of the Chinese government when the war was over. A second consideration was the matter of extraterritoriality. He had ascertained after a lengthy correspondence with Lord Derby that the benefit of extraterritoriality under the treaty with China applied only on terra firma and not on board Chinese ships of war, and he disliked the possibility of British officers and a British crew being subject to Chinese law.

The two vessels set out on their hazardous journey at the end of July 1876 and it took them over four months to reach Tientsin. They were detained at Aden, owing to a furious wind with a heavy following sea, and had the monsoon against them all the way from Singapore. They were the first two vessels of the kind ever to have made such a voyage and the British Admiralty was startled at what it considered a great achievement. Twice they had been nearly stopped, at Malta by the British admiral, who had half a mind to detain them as he believed they were pirates, and then at Manila, where they gave some trouble to the Spanish authorities. But fortunately the captains had been provided by Campbell with papers from the Board of Trade, so that all ended happily. Hart went down to Tientsin to receive the vessels and hand them over to Li Hung-chang, who was delighted to know that in them the Chinese government had the most powerful gunboats afloat. "You have managed admirably," wrote Cartwright to Campbell, "and the translation of all your despatches will show the Chinese how much care has been taken in every particular."

Meanwhile, the *Gamma* and *Delta*, with many little improvements, were getting ready for their trials, and these two vessels went out in the spring of

1877 under the command of Captain William M. Lang of the British navy. They arrived at Foochow in June and Cartwright wrote from that port: "The Chinese are much pleased with them and are full of praise for the satisfactory and minute way in which you do business. The Governor told me that he wanted to order 4 more of the same size and through the same channels. What a nice fellow Lang is! . . . Admiral Ting spoke in handsome terms of your services and has written to Li suggesting that you be specially recommended for some mark of the Imperial favour." Campbell's services were indeed so much appreciated by the Chinese that the news got abroad that he was to be China's first consul-general in England. The *Glasgow Herald* of 30 March 1877 contained the following editorial note:

> I understand that the Chinese Government is so pleased with the energy and tact displayed by Mr Campbell, who in this country acts as the representative of Mr Hart, the superintendent of the Chinese Customs Department, that it has been notified to Mr Campbell through the Ambassador that he will be appointed Consul General for the Celestial Empire. Mr Campbell was originally in the Treasury and subsequently in the Audit Office. Some twelve years ago he was appointed Private Secretary to Mr Lay, then just commencing the system of collecting the Customs duties in China for the Imperial Government. After a few years' residence in the East, Mr Campbell returned to this country and was confirmed in his post as agent here by Mr Hart, who had succeeded to Mr Lay. Mr Campbell has displayed great activity in getting the gunboats recently furnished to the Chinese Government fitted in the best style and after the most approved models; and it is not too much to say that the result of his energy, carried into effect by the Elswick Iron Company, will be not only to give the Chinese Government a very different naval position than they have hitherto occupied, but also to revolutionise in a great measure naval architecture of our smaller ocean-going vessels of war.

The rumour of this appointment was wrong however; Campbell preferred to remain as and where he was.

An interesting despatch from Campbell to Hart of October 1877 shows that Armstrong's offered him a commission of four and a half per cent in respect of the purchase of the four gunboats, which he very properly refused to take. And as a further instance of his moral rectitude it may be mentioned that some time previously he had felt it his duty, since he was acting in a fiduciary capacity as China's agent, to surrender a large block of shares which he held in the firm. As the shares subsequently increased greatly in value, he thereby deprived himself of a great chance of making money, but clearly it was the right thing to do.

In 1878 Li Hung-chang asked for another four gunboats and these went out in the summer of 1879, again under the command of Captain Lang. They were known as the "epsilon" class and Li was highly pleased with them. I shall leave it to Lang himself to describe his reception by the viceroy, in a letter he wrote from Tientsin on 30 November 1879, on board H.I.C.M.S. *Chin pei* (Defender of the north), earlier called *Epsilon:*

> When the Viceroy heard that we had come up from Taku in 6½ hours against tide, he was much pleased . . . Three days after Mr Hart came down from Peking, and walked round the Epsilon, and on the 27th the transfer of the vessels to the Chinese Government took place. Mr Hart and Admiral Ting stepped on board at noon as the flags were being exchanged . . . The French Captain of the Lynx and myself have just had a battle on paper, "Ironclads versus Epsilons." He had taken the trouble to inform the Viceroy that the gunboats will be of very little use. I take 4 gunboats and thrash the Ironclad . . . The interview with the Viceroy lasted about 2 hours. Upon departing he shook me very warmly by the hand, unusual with the Chinese, I fancy . . . I can only trust I have given you satisfaction. After all your kindness to me I cannot take too deep an interest in the work you entrusted to me.

It may be said, *en passant*, that the French at this time were beginning to be jealous of the growing English influence in Chinese naval affairs; after all, it was a Frenchman, Prosper Giquel, who had founded the Foochow Arsenal and built the Chinese Southern Fleet.

The viceroy pressed Lang to take a permanent post under him, but Lang refused, making Li rather angry by saying that he would accept the appointment only if it came through Hart. Certain French officers were put in command instead, and according to Lang they did none too well. He wrote from H.M.S. *Kestrel*, Canton, in January 1880, "I hear that Li-Hung-Chang is not quite happy in his retention of French naval officers that are now filling the post he offered me." Lang really was interested in taking command of the new fleet, especially as it was now to be strengthened by the addition of more gunboats and of two powerful cruisers which Campbell had ordered from

Armstrong's. From the *Kestrel*, Hong Kong, in June 1880, he wrote: "I would very much like to take command of the fleet, for I believe with patience you can make a very good sailor out of John Chinaman, that is by recruiting from the fishing population, and the vessels you are sending out next year will make a most powerful fleet. They are the most perfect fighting machines that have ever been designed . . . I would give anything to command vessels of your new cruiser type." He persisted, however, in declining any appointment from the Chinese government unless it came through Hart, and he informed the British Admiralty accordingly. I rather stress this point, because Paul King, who had something of a prejudice against Hart, tries to make out in his book that Lang preferred to serve China direct rather than through Hart.

The success which had attended Campbell's efforts was so much appreciated in China that the Canton viceroy approached him during 1880 with regard to the rearmament of the Southern Fleet, but nothing came of it beyond the ordering of some armaments and Martini-Henry rifles. Campbell insisted on the money being at once forthcoming, but with an insurrection in Hainan and general distress throughout the provinces, the provincial treasuries were empty.

A new batch of gunboats (the "iota" squadron) went out in 1881. Lang himself was unable to take them out, but he met them on their arrival at Hong Kong in August, and wrote to Campbell: "I see many little improvements. I hope you will receive the kudos you deserve for making these powerful little vessels such perfect fighting machines. The Gamma class cannot be compared with the Epsilon class as fighting and seagoing vessels." The new cruisers followed shortly afterwards, and the fleet, which in the following year was to be still further strengthened by ironclads ordered from Stettin, was now fast becoming the most powerful in the Pacific, making Lang say, "I wish we had the Chinese fleet instead of the English fleet when the 2 new cruisers come out."

The cruisers, unlike the gunboats, went out under the Chinese flag. Admiral Ting Ju-ch'ang himself came over to fetch them, bringing Chinese crews with him. Ting, who was one of Li Hung-chang's protégés, did not know much about ships himself, having been in the past a military official, but he had the assistance of Captain Clayson, an English officer who had served in the fleet for some time. The Chinese crews caused no little stir on their arrival

at Newcastle, and the rumour got about that they had come as dock labourers
to supplant British labour. A demonstration was got up in London by the
notorious Mr H. M. Hyndman, leader of the newly formed Social Democratic
Federation. Paul King, who was serving in the London office at the time, was
sent by Campbell to explain matters to Hyndman. Mr Hyndman was at first
obstinate, but when King told him that he was coming to the meeting himself
and that if Hyndman did not tell his audience the truth, he would, Hyndman
decided that discretion was the better part of valour, and not a word about
the Chinese was uttered.

The appointment of a foreign organiser for the new fleet remained to be
settled. America, Germany, and France were all eager to have the appointment for one of their nationals, and it was for a long time doubtful who would
be successful. Hart himself pressed for Lang. His long experience of foreign
jealousies and intrigues in Peking gave him reason to fear that if a "foreigner"
—particularly a German—was appointed, he would rapidly abuse his position
in the interest of his own country, whereas a Britisher, he thought, might be
trusted to pursue an enlightened "cosmopolitan" policy, aiming at the greatest good of all and doing harm to none. The great difficulty in Lang's case
was that England, unlike other countries, would not allow one of her officers
to serve a foreign country in time of war against a "civilised" power. Hart's
private letters written to Campbell at this time show a bitter disappointment
at England's weakness and falling prestige in the East. I quote a striking passage from one of the letters: "I want to make China strong and I want her to
make England her best friend. English doings—Consular always and Legation
occasionally—are against me, and the doings of other Powers are of a nature
to quintuple the depths of the English suicide."

Nevertheless, Lang was the ultimate choice, although a difficulty arose
at the last moment, for Lang, despite his former eagerness, showed a reluctance
to accept, fearing that his prospects of promotion in the British navy might
be damaged, and Campbell had to approach the Admiralty for an assurance
on the point. Finally Lang yielded to Hart's strong pressure, and I find the
following in a letter written by him to Campbell in November 1882: "At last
I am in the harness of the Chinese Government. I had 3 or 4 interviews with
Li Hung Chang when at Tientsin and received my appointment on the 8th of
this month as Inspector General of the Fleet (Northern Navy) with the rank

of Vice-Admiral. To organise will be very up-hill work as there will be many evils to clear away and there is at present but a very poor personnel. There are very few officers and many of these but of little use."

While all this agitation about the appointment had been going on, the new Chinese fleet had done some good work and had thoroughly frightened the Japanese. A revolution had broken out in Korea, caused by Japan's "knavish tricks"; China had sent some troops to restore order in this, her vassal state, and these had been opposed by Japanese troops. Admiral Ting promptly set forth with his gunboat fleet to Korea, reinstated the king, and brought his usurping uncle (Japan's protégé) to Tientsin as a prisoner. Thus Japan received what the press of the time called "a regular slap in the face." Japan had then only one ironclad that could keep the sea, and the opinion expressed in naval circles was that her fleet would have been easily smashed by China's up-to-date vessels. Friends of China were jubilant and Campbell received many congratulatory letters. Lady Hart wrote him in September 1882: "If people in Europe fully appreciated the action of China in the Corean difficulty they would not fail to admire and be astonished at the rapidity and efficiency with which the sleepy old celestials acted. With having been so much identified with the gunboats, I am sure you will be delighted to hear of their having done such good service."

Lang soon got the fleet into very good order, but his first command did not last very long. In the late spring of 1884, disappointed at what he thought was the British Admiralty's neglect of him (during the Egyptian crisis some of his juniors had been promoted over his head) and nervous as to what his position might be in the event of war between China and France over the Tongking boundary, he resigned. As events turned out, war was never formally declared between the two countries and the Northern Fleet was not called upon to take any action. But there was a good deal of fighting, nevertheless, and in October 1884 the Chinese Southern Fleet, while lying totally unprepared in Pagoda Anchorage at Foochow, was rather brutally attacked and destroyed by France's Admiral Amédé Courbet.

Following Lang's resignation, German officers were put in charge of the Northern Fleet, but like the French officers before them, they do not seem to have given much satisfaction. Lang was not absent for long, however, and soon after the French business had been settled in the remarkable fashion described later in this memoir, he rejoined the fleet and received a rapturous welcome from Admiral Ting. I shall leave him once again to describe in his own words his reception by the viceroy. He wrote to Campbell at the beginning of 1886:

> The Chinese appear to be heartily sick of the Germans. Military as well as Naval men are leaving, I hear . . . I met with a very cordial reception from the Viceroy, who shook me by the hand when he entered the Council Chamber, and also when I left, seeing me through a labyrinth of passages to the entrance of the Yamen on my taking leave of him . . . He was very complimentary and told me that it was owing to the petition of Admiral Ting and the officers of the squadron, with which he heartily sympathised, that he requested the British Government to sanction my return to China.

Lang signalised his return by taking the fleet to Korea and Vladivostok, where, to use his own words, "We astonished the Russians by our fine fleet and by what we did when there."

Three more cruisers with gunboats and torpedo boats were sent out by Campbell in 1888, by which time Lang had brought the fleet to a high state of efficiency. Lang found the men themselves splendid material and formed as high an opinion of the Chinese sailor as General Gordon previously had of the Chinese soldier. He had a poor opinion of the officers, however, and used often to complain of the difficulty he had in obtaining proper supplies. Lang's letters to Campbell indeed consist largely of an indictment of the Chinese official and middle classes. Here are some extracts:

> I find it very difficult to obtain proper supplies. Everything that is sanctioned is done just as if it was conferring on me a special favour . . . I beg and pray for ammunition and stores and more ships. The Viceroy replies that he cannot get the people in Peking to do anything. There is no money. He tells me that I am too anxious to get everything at once.

> The men are good, very good, but they have such poor officers, such a poor example to look up to.

> We can make anything of the men, but the officers are as a rule lazy and I have hard work to keep them at theirs.

> It is very sickening to observe the want of patriotism in these high officials. They all work for their own ends and care not a straw for the

defence of their country. Their main thought is "How much can I squeeze out of the sums given to provide for the defence of the Empire." He used to complain of the Chinese admiralty board of "old women," referring no doubt to its president, Prince Ch'un, the seventh prince, and Marquis Tseng, both old and ailing men, and he had a special dislike of officials like a taotai named Chou, a man, he said, "who is quite ignorant of naval matters and knows not a mast from a pennant, and yet poses before the Prince and the Admiralty Board as an authority."

Lang was a born grumbler and a hot-tempered one at that, but there is no doubt that he was justified in some of his complaints. At the same time he was proud of his fleet and used often to boast that, under Admiral Ting, for whom he had a great admiration, he was prepared to take on and beat any fleet of equivalent numbers. And even after some of his most scathing indictments we find remarks like these:

> During our annual prize firing the other day, the Chih Yuan with her 21 c. m. gun, mounted on Vavasseur control pivot, fired 4 shells in 6 minutes, steaming 8 knots past the target at 1600 yards and made 3 direct hits.

> Our training is going on very well indeed. We had our annual prize firing the other day with big guns and the practice was excellent. Steaming past a target at 8 knots and parallel to it, distance 1700 yards, several direct hits were recorded and from our 21 c. m. guns 5 rounds were fired in 6 minutes.

This postscript to a letter written in October 1888 is also of interest:

> Some use was made of our men the other day in Formosa. The hill tribes and settlers revolted and the troops could not do anything but lost many of their number. Ting with the Chih [Yuan] and Ching Yuan were ordered down and they landed 20 men and a 6 in. field piece which they worked well and drove the rebels back defeating them with loss. The soldiers are a lazy opium smoking lot of ruffians.

Lang's second command lasted about five years. In August 1890, peeved at what he considered a slight to his dignity by the Chinese second in command during Admiral Ting's absence, he resigned in a huff. The viceroy stupidly made no attempt to retain him, despite strong efforts by Gustav Detring, the famous commissioner at Tientsin who for long was considered the viceroy's bosom friend. Detring went with Lang to take leave of the viceroy and

50

made the latter very angry by prophesying that within a year, if his fleet was required for service, there would be a good chance of the Pagoda Anchorage incident of 1884 being repeated. And so it turned out, for after Lang's departure the fleet rapidly deteriorated, and, as Bland and Backhouse narrate in their fascinating book on the Empress Dowager,* all the money which should have gone to it was most iniquitously diverted by the chief eunuch to the rebuilding of the Summer Palace. The result of it all was that when a war with Japan broke out four years later, in 1894, the fleet went into action with practically no ammunition on board and did not stand a chance against the efficient and well-equipped Japanese fleet. For those like Campbell who had done so much to build up the Chinese fleet it was pitiful to reflect that, had that fleet remained in the condition it was in under Lang's command, the less powerful Japanese fleet must surely have been defeated. But the crafty Japanese, who had carefully studied everything beforehand, were of course aware of the rot that had set in and knew that there could only be one end to the conflict.

Towards the end of 1894 Campbell approached Lang about going out to China again and wrote him the following letter:

My dear Captain Lang,

If I have not written to you before to offer my congratulations on your new appointment, it is because I have been very busy and am very anxious too in the present state of affairs. The Chinese must feel now what a mistake they made in letting you go; and I should not be surprised if they were to ask you to go back to them when the war is over, and allow you free scope in every way. They will have to rebuild their navy and they will require an experienced adviser whom they can trust. I hope he may be an Englishman, and, if an Englishman, I hope he may be yourself.

I should like to know privately, whether you would be inclined to go out again and upon what terms and conditions you would go. Do you think the Admiralty would allow you to accept an appointment, the position and authority being such as was satisfactory to yourself?

It is impossible to say when the war will be over, and much may depend upon the next battle and the movements of the Japs if they are

---

*J. O. P. Bland and E. Backhouse, *China under the Empress Dowager* (Philadelphia, Lippincott, 1911).

victorious. If China is determined to fight it out, she ought to win and, I think, must win. I do not think the Japs have many friends here, and they will become overbearing unless China gives them a thrashing sooner or later.

Lang, however, did not see his way to throwing up a high appointment he had now obtained in the British navy (he was shortly to become admiral) and he wrote to Campbell in November 1894:

It was kind and thoughtful of you to think of this for me. I hope Sir Robert will not be very disappointed. There are quite as good men as myself who would not decline such a splendid offer. I wish I was free to do so as I feel sure now that there would be some result for energy given.

They are a peculiar people to serve with but now I know them it is not so difficult to manage them. The rough ground has been ploughed over and scraped small. I would never go through again what I experienced when I had to fight with all the corrupt officials and my own intriguing surroundings nor would I ask any one else to go through it. The work would be very easy now as I am very conversant with it all and know so well the character of officers and men.

Thus ended Campbell's connection with the Chinese fleet and with Admiral Lang. He had done his best for China, and all would have been well if the Chinese had entrusted the finance and general management of the fleet to the one sound administrative body in China, the Customs Service, and if they had made an energetic and capable man like Cartwright secretary to the admiralty, as Lang himself so often strongly urged. As it was, a splendid fleet went to ruin simply because of the corruption which prevailed among the higher Chinese officials of half a century ago.

The Chinese government early expressed its appreciation of Campbell's work in connection with the fleet by conferring upon him the first two of the many decorations he was subsequently to receive from it. He received in 1878 by imperial decree the civil rank of the Third Class (Blue Button) and in 1882 the civil rank of the Second Class (Red Button).

VIII

THE INTERNATIONAL EXHIBITIONS

In 1851 Prince Albert launched his great international exhibition in Hyde Park (ten years later, shortly before his death, he had another planned). It was always the endeavour of that kindly man to encourage friendly relations between the nations, and the international exhibition was one of the means by which he sought to bring this about and dissipate, as he fondly hoped, all thoughts of war. But it takes something more than an international exhibition to overcome the fighting instincts of man, and the prince's hopes of peace were sadly frustrated. Within scarcely twenty years two major wars had broken out (not to count the Indian Mutiny and the American Civil War), and in addition there were several minor wars, of which one was Britain's inexcusable war with China over the lorcha *Arrow*. After the Franco-German War of 1870, however, the ball which the prince consort had started was set rolling again, and between 1873 and 1885 there followed a regular procession of international exhibitions, in all of which China, anxious to show the importance she attached to the maintenance and extension of friendly relations with the powers, took an active part. The work on each of these occasions, with the single exception of the Amsterdam exhibition, was entrusted by the Chinese government to Hart, and in nearly all of them Campbell took an active part.

First came the Vienna exhibition of 1873. Campbell was one of the four commissioners who represented China, and at the end of it he received from the emperor of Austria the first of his foreign decorations. In the Philadelphia exhibition of 1876 he took no part. The three commissioners selected to represent China were James Hart, the I.G.'s brother, Hammond, and Hunter, and from all accounts China's display was successful and interesting. Then came the Paris exhibition of 1878. Hart himself came over on this occasion, his last visit to Europe, as it turned out, until his final departure from China in 1908. Campbell, who managed all the preliminary work in Europe, was his second in command, the other commissioners being Glover, Novion, and Colin Jamieson. The Chinese Court was one of the great attractions of the exhibition, as was the Chinese Pavilion at the Trocadero, which had been specially built by Chinese labour to the design of Lung Ling-king, the best builder and archi-

tect in China. For his part in this Paris exhibition Campbell received the first
of his French decorations, being made an Officer of the Legion of Honour.

In the exhibitions in Berlin in 1880 and Amsterdam in 1883 Campbell
appears to have taken no part, but in the three London exhibitions which
followed (Fisheries, Health, and Inventions—all of them held in the spacious
vacant land, now long since built over, which used to be to the south of the
Albert Hall) he was, quite naturally, China's "chief performer."

The invitation to China to take part in the Fisheries Exhibition had
arrived rather late in the day, but, owing to the energy displayed by Hart and
the international team of Customs officials he had selected (Neumann, German;
Morgan, English; Drew, American; Novion, French) all difficulties of collection
and transport were swiftly overcome. As a result the Chinese exhibit created
a great sensation and was on several occasions warmly commended by the
press. Shortly before the opening of the exhibition, the *Times* commented:
"To the surprise of everyone, China has been the first nation to put in an
appearance at the exhibition. But when it is known that Sir Robert Hart, the
I.G. of Chinese Customs, acting under the instructions of the Chinese Government, undertook only in September last the preparation of the collection in
China, and that Mr Campbell, his representative in London, has made arrangements for its instalment here, only one more proof is afforded of the efficiency
of the European Customs Service as a department of the Chinese Government."
On 15 May 1883 the *Times* gave a long account of the opening, in which the
following appeared:

> Their Royal Highnesses the Duke and Duchess of Connaught paid a
> long visit to the Chinese Court, where they were received by Mr J. D.
> Campbell, one of the Commissioners for the Imperial Maritime Customs
> Department of China . . . It will be generally admitted, if not without
> some feeling of surprise, that the Chinese collection is perhaps the most
> remarkable, and certainly if taken as a whole, the most instructive
> section in the Exhibition. It is also the most artistically worked out . . .

Then followed details about the various exhibits and remarks on the excellence
of Chinese methods employed both for capturing and for breeding fish, which
had anticipated by many generations those in vogue in Europe.

The Chinese Court, of which I have a large framed photograph, was
indeed universally recognized as the most attractive of the exhibits, and at the
end China was awarded seven gold medals and one diploma. The medals were

for fish, nets, fishing gear, boats, shells, the system of lights on the coast, and a special medal for the court and its surroundings. The diploma was for the collection of crabs! Campbell read to a conference of experts a learned paper on the fisheries of China, which was afterwards printed as part of the exhibition literature. He finished his labours by obtaining the acceptance of the Chinese exhibits by the Prince of Wales. The prince selected a few objects for himself and presented the remainder to the South Kensington Museum. I notice that Campbell, when sending to Sir Philip Cunliffe Owen the draft of his letter to the prince's private secretary, displayed his usual modesty, disclaiming all credit for himself. "Of course," he said, "Sir Robert Hart is the *real* person who has done everything, and it is on his advice that the Chinese Government place the Exhibit at the disposal of the Prince of Wales." Lady Hart, however, knew better; she was now permanently residing in England, and I give extracts from two of her letters to Campbell:

14 Oct. 1883. I do not know how to thank you for having mentioned my husband in connection with honorary distinctions. I am aware and tell him also very often that you never let him be overlooked, and I feel that he and I have no truer or loyal friend than yourself. If any distinctions are distributed, I hope you will not be forgotten, for I think you merit one as much if not more than anyone else.

5 Nov. 1883. I can honestly congratulate you on the success of the Chinese Court which was entirely due to your personal exertions, taste and tact. The Prince of Wales' gracious acceptance of the Collection was the crowning point, and, as far as I have been able to make out, everything has been couleur de rose. I was greatly pleased with your article in the Chinese Telegraph. In a word I am sure it is a gem in the collection of literature on the subject.

The Fisheries Exhibition over, a health exhibition, mainly intended to illustrate the food supply of the different countries, was proposed for the following year, and in September of 1883 Campbell wrote to Cunliffe Owen urging that, if China was to take part, the official invitation should be sent to the Chinese government as soon as possible so as to enable adequate preparations. "I suppose there is no country in the world," he wrote, "which has a more extensive cuisine than China; and if we could get over a few good cooks and some Chinese boys to act as waiters, the Chinese restaurant ought to be the chef d'oeuvre of the Exhibition, and it should pay all expenses."

The invitation was sent, and China's display at the Health Exhibition was even more impressive than her display at the fishing exhibit had been. The Chinese Court was again considered to be the most attractive of the exhibits, not excepting "Old London"; the restaurant advocated by Campbell was housed in a building specially erected for it, and, to add to the gaiety of nations, a Chinese band came over too. When it first arrived this band could only play Chinese music, which, though regarded by some experts as akin to the music of ancient Greece, grated strangely on English ears. But under the guidance of Dr Wilde, Gresham Professor of Music and head of the London Academy of Music, the band speedily mastered most of the popular English airs and, of course, the various national anthems, and its daily performances in a Chinese pavilion built over an artificial lake were warmly cheered by admiring audiences. The rehearsals were frequently held at our house, and I remember well the weird instruments that were used, some of them obvious anticipations of our modern stringed instruments. The many Chinese who accompanied the exhibition were well looked after. They were so grateful to Campbell for his kindness to them that before they left they presented him with an album of their photographs and an illuminated address in Chinese with an English translation thus rather touchingly and gracefully worded:

As some of us are about to leave London on our return to China, we trust you will allow us to offer you this Album, containing our photographs, as a token of respect and gratitude for all you have done for us while in this great City. From the moment we landed here up to the present time you have been unremitting in your care for our comfort and enjoyment, and on our return to our own land we shall tell our compatriots how well we have been treated and how much we have seen. In taking leave of you, we wish you and Mrs Campbell and all your children, good health, long life and happiness. We hope it may be our good fortune to meet you once more, but, if we should never come to Europe again, we can assure you that we shall never forget you.

October, 1884

In the last of the South Kensington exhibitions, Inventions, the part taken by China was less impressive. No Chinese came over, and things had been made difficult owing to the war between China and France, the peace negotiations occupying Campbell's whole attention for the first part of 1885 and keeping him in Paris. So far as modern mechanical inventions were concerned,

China of course had little or nothing to show; her great inventions had related to the past. All the same, China's past mechanical inventiveness came as a great surprise. The most the average Englishman of those days knew about China was that in a remote past she had introduced the cultivation of tea, the production of silk, and the manufacture of porcelain. He was amazed to find that in the distant centuries when the English and other European nationals were mere savages China, to mention only a few of her mechanical achievements, had invented a chariot containing a figure which always pointed south (thus anticipating the modern compass in a reverse direction), had invented a machine for showing the distance travelled, and had introduced the art of printing from wood blocks.

When the last of these exhibitions was over, the Prince of Wales was again asked to accept what remained of the exhibits, and here is the letter which Sir Julian Pauncefote addressed to Campbell from the Foreign Office in December 1885:

Dear Mr Campbell,

Lord Salisbury desires me to inform you that the thanks of His Royal Highness the Prince of Wales as President of the Exhibition, and those of Her Majesty's Government, will be conveyed to the Chinese Government through Her Majesty's Representative at Peking, to whom instructions on the subject will be sent both by Telegraph and Post, for their friendly cooperation in the Fisheries, Health and Inventions Exhibitions, as also for the Chinese Exhibits at Kensington which have been accepted by His Royal Highness.

Lord Salisbury has read with much satisfaction the address presented to you by the Chinese sent over to this Country in connection with the Exhibits of China, in which they express their acknowledgments for the great kindness and attention they received at your hands.

I am,
Dear Mr Campbell,
Yours very truly,
J. Pauncefote

So ended the great South Kensington exhibitions. There are some people who belittle the contribution which international exhibitions can make towards the fostering of international amity, but, so far as China was concerned, it may safely be said that much good resulted. The ignorance of most Englishmen about China and everything Chinese had been simply colossal, but these three exhibitions, at any rate in the case of those who were fortunate enough to see them, did something to remove this ignorance, and Englishmen began to look upon China with greater appreciation and with more friendly eyes.

For his part in these three exhibitions Campbell neither sought nor obtained recognition. With that innate modesty which Lord Rendel calls his "one honourable defect" he was content that all the credit should go to his chief, Sir Robert Hart.

IX

CAMPBELL AS A DIPLOMAT
THE FRENCH AND PORTUGUESE TREATIES, 1885 AND 1887

The French Treaty

In 1883 hostilities broke out between France and China over Tongking, and it ultimately fell to Campbell's lot to negotiate with M. Jules Ferry, France's prime minister, the treaty of peace between the two countries. It was a work which he regarded as the most important of his whole career.

Before I begin the story of the negotiations, a few words should be said about the rise of French power in the Far East and the events which led up to the crisis. Defeated in India, France during the last half of the eighteenth century had resolutely sought means to re-establish her own power in the East and counterbalance that of England. She saw her opportunity in the political condition of the decadent kingdom of Annam. In 1787 she obtained from the king of Annam, in return for aid given him by French troops, the concession of some territory on his eastern coast. As time went on, her influence in this area increased, and in 1862, fired by the enthusiasm of Emperor Napoleon III, one of whose dreams was a powerful French empire in the East, she acquired from the king the greater part of Cochin China. This was followed the next year (1863) by the granting of a protectorate over Cambodia. After the war with Germany, France resumed her activities in the East. In 1874, anxious to secure a better trade route to China's rich southern provinces of Yunnan and Szechwan, she secured another treaty with the king of Annam under which the Red River was opened to trade, together with the cities of Haiphong and Hanoi on its delta.

The king of Annam, however, was now beginning to be seriously alarmed at these encroachments on his domain and, suddenly remembering that he was a tributary of China, appealed to his suzerain lord, the emperor of China, for protection. (Campbell received an interesting account of an appeal made in 1882 in a letter from Gustav Detring written on 27 September 1882.)** China thereupon protested to France, claiming that Annam was her vassal state. She made the protest with some vigour, for at the time she was buoyed up by a satisfactory treaty that she had recently concluded with Russia over

her western frontier and by the success obtained this very year against Japan
and Korea, mainly owing to the action taken by her Northern Fleet.

France made light of the protest, and as Tongking was infested by pirates
she sent troops to restore order. These were opposed by Chinese irregular
troops known as the "Black Flags," who received secret assistance from the
Chinese government, and the French met with some reverses, losing a general
or two. Jules Ferry, who had become French prime minister early in 1883, at
once determined on a vigorous forward policy. The greatest Frenchman of
his age, he believed that in colonial expansion—in Asia, Africa, and Madagas-
car—was to be found France's means of recovering the prestige she had lost
in her war with Germany, and he regarded the acquisition of Tongking as
indispensable to the preservation of Cochin China. Proceeding on the then
generally accepted political maxim, "Might is Right," he succeeded in August
1883 in forcing the king of Annam to conclude another treaty under which
a French protectorate over Annam and Tongking was recognised.

China was not disposed to accept this new development, and Li Hung-
chang, who was negotiating the matter on her behalf, had the greatest difficulty in controlling the war party, now rapidly coming to the fore. A letter
from Customs commissioner Alfred E. Hippisley to Campbell, of 26 July
1883,** gave an informative picture of the situation. Not satisfied with Li's
efforts to arrive at a peaceful and dignified solution, the Chinese government
withdrew the negotiations from Li's control and placed them in the hands of
their minister in London, the more warlike Marquis Tseng. But if Detring's
account of Tseng's proceedings (in a letter to Campbell of 19 January 1884)**
is true, Tseng made matters rather worse than better by throwing over the
moderate proposals of the more conciliatory Li and claiming from France
more than she was prepared to yield. The relations between Li and the marquis
became strained in consequence, and France eagerly seized the opportunity
to play off the two rival statesmen against each other.

What exactly happened after this is not clear, but Li seems again to have
taken charge, for on 11 May 1884 he signed at Tientsin with Captain Fournier,
a French naval officer and the authorised French representative, a convention
under which France agreed to recognise China's sovereign rights, and China
on her part undertook to recognise the French protectorate and withdraw
her troops from northern Tongking. Unfortunately no procedure was drawn

up for the withdrawal of the Chinese troops, so that in June 1884, when the French proceeded to occupy the frontier town of Langson, the Chinese general refused to evacuate on the grounds that he had received no official instructions. The French thereupon rashly attacked and were defeated with severe loss at a place called Bac-li. The fat was now in the fire. The French demanded a big indemnity for the affront, China refused to pay, and hostilities were renewed.

It was soon after this that China, having failed to reach any agreement through her own diplomats, and at her wit's end to know how to act, turned to Hart to get them out of the impasse. Hart's first step was to go to Shanghai in order to get into touch with M. Patenôtre, the French representative there. After discussion with him, he proposed that China should agree to pay an indemnity of four million taels. The Tsungli Yamen refused, and Hart returned to Peking. His first effort had failed dismally.

Hart took time to consider his next step. Through the agency of Campbell he was being kept constantly informed as to public sentiment in France and Europe. It so happened that William Cartwright, one of the ablest men in the Customs Service, was at home. Campbell sent him to Paris to report all events of any importance, and a bundle of letters that he wrote to Campbell from Paris between July and September of 1884 has been preserved.** They show that Paris was in almost as great a state of bewilderment as Peking and that feeling changed from day to day if not from hour to hour. At one moment it favoured mediation, at another it did not; one day the cabinet would send orders to its fleet to proceed to extremes, the next day it would suspend the order; always insistent on the payment of an indemnity, the cabinet would at one time reduce, at another increase the amount.

It was during Cartwright's stay in Paris, on 23 August to be exact, that, although war had not yet been formally declared, the French fleet under Admiral Courbet entered Foochow harbour and without any warning mercilessly destroyed in a few brief minutes the whole of the antiquated Chinese Southern Fleet as it lay totally unprepared at anchor. It was an act which was not to the taste of many Frenchmen, and the head of the French admiralty himself informed Cartwright that it was not to his liking: "Cà nous embête," he said. Admiral Courbet then proceeded to occupy Keelung on Formosa and to blockade the whole of the Chinese southern coast. Infiltrations were also undertaken on land. Here the French were not always so successful, and on several occasions the Chinese troops fully justified the high opinion of their fighting capabilities which General Gordon had formed some years back.

French action had now become injurious to neutrals. There was some risk that Britain might become implicated, that Chinese administration might break up, and that other powers, particularly Russia and Japan, might take occasion to pursue territorial projects. If further international complications were to be avoided something had to be done soon.

Cartwright, in one of his last Paris letters to Campbell, had suggested that, since Paris was becoming more favourable to the idea of mediation, the best thing that could happen would be for England and Germany to propose the mediation of the United States. Hart seized on this suggestion and on 11 September sent a telegram to Campbell with a confidential message for Stuart Rendel. It requested Rendel to see Lord Granville, the British foreign secretary, and attempt to arrange that the British and German governments invite the French and Chinese governments to submit to the arbitration of the United States. Rendel was chosen for two reasons. As one of Gladstone's friends he enjoyed exceptional means and opportunities of making the necessary representations to Lord Granville. Secondly, he had some considerable acquaintance with China, gained chiefly from the part he had taken, as a partner in Armstrong's, in supplying gunboats and cruisers for the Northern Fleet. Moreover, he was on terms of close and friendly association with Campbell.

Rendel at once got into touch with Lord Granville, being careful to consult Campbell at every stage. In fact, during the last four months of 1884 hardly a day passed when he did not visit or write to Campbell. The latter, with what Lady Hart described as his "usual good taste, tact and discretion," did not see Lord Granville himself, but he was all the time in close touch with the French ambassador M. Waddington. In the result of all this Lord Granville did make some attempt to bring about mediation, but by the end of December his efforts had proved abortive and both he and Rendel subsequently dropped completely out of the picture. Hart's second indirect attempt had therefore failed.

Twice disappointed, Hart now conceived the idea of negotiating directly with M. Ferry himself, through the agency of Campbell. (The situation by then had become even more serious, for, to the annoyance of neutrals, France decided to declare the rice on which northern China so much depended a contraband of war, and she also threatened to send an army of 50,000 men to Peking.) The negotiations that ensued were perhaps the most extraordinary that have ever happened in diplomatic history; indeed they were so extraordinary that when the news got abroad that a treaty between two great powers had been brought about in this manner no one would at first believe it, and leading English newspapers like the *Times* and *Standard* professed themselves as sceptical.

The negotiations opened in a curious manner. The Chinese Customs lighthouse vessel, the *Feihoo*, had been seized by the French in November 1884 for violating the blockade of Formosa. Hart remonstrated with Admiral Courbet, who told him that if its release was required he should approach M. Ferry directly. Campbell was thereupon instructed by Hart to proceed to Paris. On 10 January 1885, notwithstanding the state of hostilities, he was received most courteously by M. Ferry, who said he would inquire at the admiralty and see what could be done. He asked him to call again in a fortnight's time. During the conversation Campbell explained to M. Ferry the difficulties which French action was causing to the Chinese Customs administration and ascertained from him that he was sincerely anxious to arrive at a peaceful solution as soon as possible. Campbell at once wired to Hart of Ferry's friendly attitude, and a plan of campaign was decided upon.

Accordingly, when Campbell resumed his conversation with M. Ferry on 24 January, he asked him, as previously arranged between him and Hart, whether he would allow the general question of the war to be discussed. Ferry assented and, after a long conversation, authorised Campbell to inform Hart that he would be prepared to consider a proposition from him, but only if it had the authority of the Tsungli Yamen. His attitude was very natural after his experience of negotiations with Chinese diplomats of such conflicting views as Li Hung-chang and Marquis Tseng. Further conversations and telegrams between Paris and Peking followed, with the result that Ferry, satisfied that Hart had now been definitely entrusted with the sole conduct of the negotiations and that Campbell had been authorised by imperial decree to sign on behalf of China, allowed the negotiations to proceed. He also agreed with Hart's stipulation that absolute secrecy be kept and that he (Ferry) use no other intermediary.

China's proposition, carefully prepared after conversations which Hart had with the Tsungli Yamen and Campbell with Ferry, was duly communicated on 1 March and accepted in general principle. Its fundamentals were that China should agree to ratify the convention which Li Hung-chang had arranged at Tientsin on 11 May 1884; France would then give up Formosa, raise her blockade, and cease all hostilities. No explicit reference was made to an indemnity. The preliminaries being settled, the form and details of the protocol and the procedure for the withdrawal of the opposing armies remained for settlement, and these M. Ferry left to M. Billot, the director of political affairs at the French Foreign Office, to arrange in conjunction with Campbell.

For the next few weeks Billot and Campbell met every day, referring points of difficulty to Ferry and Hart respectively. The condition of secrecy was strictly observed, and no one knew what was going on behind the scenes. Lord Granville knew nothing, nor did Lord Rendel, and Sir Julian Pauncefote, the British permanent undersecretary of state, who came over to Paris at this time to attend a conference on the Suez Canal and stayed at the same hotel as Campbell, had not the slightest idea that the latter was engaged on other than purely Customs business. Many difficulties of course arose, and Campbell found it uphill work dealing with the adroit French diplomats. In particular he had the greatest trouble in persuading them to waive all claims to an indemnity, but at last all was settled and on 22 March a telegram was sent to Peking announcing the French acceptance, subject to certain minor modifications, to which it was confidently anticipated that China, after the numerous telegrams which had passed between Campbell and Hart, would at once agree.

Success seemed assured. But just as the ship was entering port a storm suddenly occurred which threatened to wreck everything. Before the Peking government had time to consider and telegraph its final acceptance, news came of two serious reverses suffered by the French troops in Tongking. Hope gave place to despondency. In Paris it was feared that China, intoxicated by this unexpected success, would wish to repudiate the treaty and continue the war; in Peking it was thought that France would wish to retrieve her defeat. Rumour, that *monstrum horrendus ingens*, exaggerated the extent of the disaster, and riots broke out in Paris, hostile crowds gathering round the Quai d'Orsay and shouting "A l'eau Ferry."

After anxiously awaiting the telegram that was so long in coming, Ferry on 30 March, now fearing the worst, went to the Chamber to ask for a further vote of credit to enable him to send out reinforcements. No sooner had he finished his speech than there followed (to quote from the obituary of Ferry which appeared in *Le Temps* of 19 March 1893) "une des scènes les plus pénibles, les plus douleureuses que le Palais Bourbon ait jamais vues." Mounting the tribune, Clemenceau declared, "Nous ne vous connaissons plus, nous ne voulons plus vous connaître. Ce ne sont pas ministres que je vois devant moi, ce sont des accusés de haute traison." Other speakers followed in similar strain, and one of them alluded in insulting terms to "the obscure negotiators without authority" whom Ferry had seen fit to employ. He was referring of course to Hart and Campbell. Ferry, with peace almost in his pocket, had nobly refrained, in accordance with his promise to Hart, from making any mention of the secret negotiations that had been going on, but somehow, during this fateful week, a distorted account of them had leaked out in one of the Paris newspapers.

All through the clamour Ferry sat with arms crossed, facing his accusers with a disdainful smile. Little did he or they know that at the very moment when all this was happening a telegram was on its way from Peking, despatched after full consideration of the French reverse, announcing China's final acceptance. The clamour subsiding, Ferry again rose and pressed for his vote of credit. He was defeated by 306 votes against 149, and thereupon he and the cabinet which had ruled France uninterruptedly for over two years, a period almost unprecedented for a French cabinet, promptly resigned.

The very next day, 31 March, the long awaited telegram arrived. It ended with a special message from Hart to Campbell, written with characteristic Irish humour, "Signez sans delai, mais ne signez pas le 1er Avril, parce que c'est un jour néfaste." Campbell, who had been specially authorized by imperial decree to sign on behalf of China, was ready to sign at once, but now another difficulty arose. Who was to sign for France? Ferry had resigned and, though still in office pending the appointment of his successor, did not feel justified in signing and thus binding the policy of the new ministry, a view with which the president, M. Jules Grévy, concurred. Hart, on being informed of this new development, wired on 1 April suggesting that M. Billot should sign, present his signature to the president, and ask him to communicate it to the Chamber. This prima facie reasonable suggestion was not accepted, and Campbell had to wire back, "Tout est en suspense mais espérons."

Hart thereupon sent two further telegrams to Campbell. In the first he said, "Le Tsung-li-yamen est très impatient d'un règlement. Un delai d'une semaine peut faire échouer l'arrangement que nous avons effectué après trois mois de travail patient et persistent. N'use de cela qu'avec discretion." In the second telegram he instructed him to write to Lord Granville confidentially stating the position, adding that intervention was still undesirable. Campbell, appreciating the position perhaps better than Hart, did not comply with this last instruction. Instead he made a last urgent appeal to Ferry himself in which he pointed out that French hesitancy was being misunderstood in China and that further delay would only be playing into the hands of China's war party, who were already being egged on by telegrams sent to them by Marquis Tseng from London. His appeal was successful. On the morning of 4 April Ferry summoned his expiring cabinet, and a unanimous decision was taken. M. Billot was sent off posthaste to the president to ask him to authorise M. Billot to sign on behalf of France. M. Billot returned with the necessary authority and at four o'clock the same afternoon he and Campbell met and signed. The haven was reached at last.

On receiving the welcome news Hart at once telegraphed to Campbell, "Bravo! Bien fait. Mes rémerciments et mes félicitations." The manner in which he communicated the success to the Tsungli Yamen is told by the late Right Honourable Sir Henry Norman in his book on the Far East, from which I quote the following: "Then Sir Robert got into his cart and went to the Tsungli Yamen. The Ministers were there and he sat down to a cup of tea with them. By and by he remarked, with the apparent indifference of the Oriental diplomat, 'It is exactly nine months today since you placed the negociations with France in my hands.' 'And the child is born!' instantly cried one of the Ministers, seeing the point and delighted at the truly Chinese way of conveying the information."*

China lost no time in ratifying the Tientsin convention of 11 May 1884, and the withdrawal of troops then proceeded regularly, according to plan. It remained to settle the definite treaty. The original intention had been that

*Henry Norman, *The Peoples and Politics of the Far East* (New York, Charles Scribner's Sons, 1895), p. 234.

this part of the work should be managed by Li Hung-chang in consultation with the French representative in China. But Charles de Freycinet, who was then minister of foreign affairs, was so impressed with the promptitude with which China was carrying out her part of the bargain and with the evident credit enjoyed by Campbell in Peking, that he asked that Campbell be allowed to stay on in Paris to settle the draft in conjunction with M. Cogordan, sub-director of foreign affairs. Permission was readily given, and for the next few weeks these two were engaged on the task, Hart being consulted when necessary.

As all the heavy spade work had already been done, the task was not too difficult, and by 23 May the text had been settled. It was cabled to Peking and after a few further alterations had been made by the French and Chinese plenipotentiaries, the treaty was finally signed at Tientsin on 9 June and formally ratified by imperial decree on June 11, 1885. At the last moment Hart had a slight tussle with M. Patenôtre, the French plenipotentiary, over the form of the imperial edict and had to write a letter to him in which he made this interesting commentary on Chinese constitutional law and custom: "Imperial Edicts are either verbal or written; and of each class there are two divisions—the decrees which are original and those which are responsive. When an Imperial Decree has to approve of something done or reported it is responsive, and its proper form is that of 'approval' of the report. To ask the Emperor now to issue another Decree is to ask him to stultify himself, and every Chinese who is told the approval is inadequate and another instrument required, will be more than astonished." M. Patenôtre climbed down and all ended happily. Just as Hart was finishing his letter to Campbell giving the news, Hart received a note that the French Legation flag was flying half-masted owing to the death of Admiral Courbet, and he enclosed the note in his letter with the red-pencilled comment, "Ferry out just as an arrangement seemed possible and Courbet dead just as the Treaty of Peace is ratified!!" Wonderment at the mysteries of Providence was characteristic of Hart, as it was also of Campbell.

The treaty ratified, commissioners were appointed (of whom James Hart was one) to delimit the frontier between Tongking and China, and M. Cogordan, at Campbell's suggestion, proceeded to China to put the finishing touches to a separate treaty of commerce which had also been prepared. Cogordan found Li Hung-chang, his Chinese opposite number, rather aggrieved at not having been asked to negotiate the preliminaries, but the two speedily became friends, and Cogordan was able to leave at the end of 1885 with his mission accomplished and with the happiest impressions of China and the Chinese.

Thus ended a remarkable chapter in the political history of France and China. In compiling the foregoing account of the Paris negotiations, I have consulted, in addition to numerous other documents and letters left behind by Campbell, the French Yellow Book, a printed memorandum correcting and supplementing the Yellow Book which was written by Campbell in April 1886 and approved by Jules Ferry, and lastly and chiefly three articles written by M. Billot which appeared in the *Revue Bleue* of December 1884 and which Jules Ferry highly commended as "une page d'histoire écrite d'un main de maître." Ferry had previously commended Campbell's own memorandum as "un tableau très fidèle des conversations toutes confidentielles qui ont précédé les pourparlers avec Sir Robert Hart. Il complète l'histoire de cette négociation qui n'a certainement ressemblé à aucune autre, mais qui s'est terminée dans des conditions de précision et de bonne volonté qui n'avait jamais offertes, à ce qu'il me semble, aucune négociation antérieure entre la Chine et l'Europe."

I have quoted these authorities because in subsequent years false statements about the negotiations were from time to time made. One was *Le Journal d'un Mandarin*, which made the absurd claim that the negotiations had started with a telegram sent by the Chinese minister in Berlin. When Campbell wrote to M. Cogordan in March 1894 asking him to ascertain who was the author of this lying statement, Cogordan replied that he was no Chinese at all but an unprincipled and unscrupulous Frenchman, writing for his own private ends. He gave his name and denounced him and his work. Another childish and utterly misleading account was given in Miss Bredon's popular biography of Sir Robert Hart. This was published in 1909, after Campbell's death, and I felt it my duty to write to Miss Bredon a letter of remonstrance.

A still later account was given in Lord Rendel's memoirs, published in 1931 many years after his death. Lord Rendel tried to make out that he (Lord Rendel) was mainly responsible for the treaty and that Campbell had occupied a minor role in the negotiations. He seems also to have thought that it was mainly owing to the backing that he and Lord Granville had given to Hart that the latter was accepted by the French and Chinese governments as negotiator! Knowing the truth, I wrote a letter of remonstrance to the editor of the book

and subsequently had some correspondence with Mr Henry Gladstone, one of
Lord Rendel's executors, who sought to make some amends by a letter in the
Times. At the time I wrote this remonstrance, I had not discovered certain
letters written by Lord Rendel to Campbell in 1885. These conclusively show
that, to put the mildest construction on his action, his memory must have
failed him when, long after the event, he compiled his memoirs in extreme
old age. As some years had passed when I came upon those letters, I regarded
the incident as closed, and I did not trouble to send copies of the letters to
Mr Gladstone. But they are of sufficient interest and importance to be included
here:

> Athenaeum Club, 16 April 1885
> My dear Mr Campbell,
>
> Only on my return last night from a fortnight's cruise at sea did I hear
> of your brilliant success. With all my heart I congratulate Sir Robert Hart
> and you on it.
>
> I should have profoundly rejoiced to have taken any part in it. The
> satisfaction of it would have lasted me for life. All the more and better
> am I able to sympathise with you at this moment and most deeply do I
> do so.
>
> But there is a special ground of satisfaction to me in your success. You
> have long taken the labouring over and yet have with the best of loyalty
> and unselfishness been quite content to be personally unremarked. It is
> therefore most agreeable to my sense of justice and fitness that you should
> wear the laurels yourself.
>
> Will you give my fullest felicitude to Mrs Campbell? I know how proud
> and pleased she must be.
>
> I sent a note to Sir Robert from Gibraltar and am now writing again to
> say how much I rejoice over his splendid services to China, to his country
> and to humanity.
>
> > Every believe me
> > Most truly yours
> > Stuart Rendel

> 16 Palace Gardens, 10 June 1885
> My dear Mr Campbell,
>
> I see the news of signature in this morning's paper and I congratulate
> you with my whole heart. Come home and have a good rest, both you
> and Mrs Campbell.

You have done a great stroke of work which will be a source of comfort and I hope honour and profit to you all your life . . . [Election news]

> Yours very truly
> Stuart Rendel

Plas Dinam, Llandinam, Montgomeryshire, 14 Sept. 1885
My dear Campbell,

I congratulate you with all my heart [over the Chinese decorations], and I thank you for sending me copies of the official letters. No one could take more pleasure from them than I do and perhaps few are in so good a position to appreciate their truth and justice.

After all you have some return for being overworked and may feel that you have not lived in vain.

To how few men in a generation can it happen to take part in such blessed peacemaking work . . . Please give Mrs Campbell my entire sympathy. It must be a rare addition to your happiness in these honours that your wife should have played so noble a part in helping you win them.

> Ever believe me, my dear Campbell
> Very sincerely yours
> Stuart Rendel

How Lord Rendel, after writing these letters, could be responsible for such opinions as he expressed years later passes comprehension!

Campbell, when recalling the negotiations in after years, used often to quote the old tag, "Peace hath her victories no less renowned than war," and what pleased him most was that he had so arranged matters that China paid no indemnity at all, though France had for long insisted on a large sum. Many thought that China would have made him a handsome monetary gift in consequence. This she never did; she bestowed upon him instead the third of his China decorations, the Imperial Order of the Double Dragon (Second Division, Second Class), an honour considered to be the equivalent of a baronetcy in England. Some years later he was promoted to the First Class of the same division. I have set out in Appendix 3 a full translation of the memorial presented by the Tsungli Yamen to the emperor on this occasion,** and I give here the emperor's reply:

> In the matter of the Treaty now concluded between China and France, both Sir Robert Hart and Mr Campbell took an active part in the negotiations which happily attained a perfectly satisfactory result. For their

services which were continuous from the commencement of the affair, we command that the expression of our Imperial satisfaction be conveyed to them. We also order that the bestowal of honours be given effect to as requested.—This from the Emperor.

France at the same time made him a Commander of the Legion of Honour. In announcing this honour Freycinet wrote to Campbell on 22 June 1885:

J'ai le plaisir de vous annoncer que le Président de la République voulant vous donner un témoignage particulier de sa haute bienveillance, vient, sur ma proposition, de vous conférer la croix de commandeur de l'ordre National de la Légion d'honneur.—Par décret du même jour, il a accordé à M. Hart, inspecteur général des douanes chinoises, la plaque de grand officier.

Il m'a été très agréable de faire valoir les titres que vous êtes acquis, vous et M. Hart, à ces distinctions, en participant l'un et l'autre, aux négociations qui ont abouti au traité de paix avec la Chine.

Before these Chinese and French distinctions had been awarded, Britain had already made him a C.M.G. for "services rendered in British interests." As compared with the later distinctions awarded by France and China, this British honour was insignificant. It is true that the C.M.G. was a greater honour in those days than it is now, but, seeing what vital issues were at stake and how narrowly a conflict which might have had European complications had been avoided, it was a paltry honour for his own country to have awarded. Lord Rendel thought so too, and he tried to get Lord Granville to recommend a K.C.M.G. But it was too late; the recommendation for a C.M.G. had already gone forward to the queen, the Gladstone government had resigned, and Lord Granville was therefore powerless to make further representations. Lord Rendel, in conveying his regret that nothing more could be done at the moment, said that he looked forward with confidence to Campbell being before long more fully honoured, especially if his case was backed by Hart.

To the indignation of Campbell's many China friends who considered that at the very least he should have been awarded a K.C.M.G., Hart made no move either then or later, and the general opinion was that Hart had deliberately kept Campbell's services (not only on this occasion but on many others) in the background, wishing to have all the credit himself. This was probably the case, for it was one of the failings of that great man to attribute all his successes to himself alone.

How different was Campbell's attitude towards Hart! Unselfishly keeping his own services in the background, he was forever seeking fresh honours for his chief. In this he was sometimes egged on by the ambitious Lady Hart, whose letter to him on this occasion was characteristically feminine. "Do you think," she wrote, "you could mention the matter of honours for my husband to Mr Stuart Rendel? I can quite understand how difficult all this kind of thing is, and I suppose there will be none of these things in the next planet, but they certainly count for something in this one."

But while he omitted to disclose to the world what Campbell had done, Hart was appreciative enough to Campbell himself, and in officially transmitting the Tsungli Yamen's dispatch which announced the imperial honours he concluded his letter thus: "Knowing better than anyone else how well you have done your work and how difficult and important it has been, I am happy to be the medium of the conveyance of such honours as the Chinese Government now confers."

Congratulations were showered upon Campbell from all quarters. Those which he perhaps valued most came from former members of the London office who were then stationed at Shanghai. Their joint letter was signed by Paul King, Hosea B. Morse, F. E. Taylor, J. R. Brazier, Alister Duncan, W. A. Kerr, H. W. Brazier, T. W. Moorhead. From many others I select the following:

9 April 1885 (from Mr Hutchins, the Customs solicitor)
Dear Mrs Campbell,
    Do not miss the description of your husband in the Daily News today. It is fine. He is famous now . . .

13 April 1885 (from Mr Cartwright)
    I am most heartily glad first of all that peace has been secured, and that it has been brought about by your agency. I consider that both you and the I.G. have achieved a brilliant success, for the difficulties were equally great in Paris and Peking. The responsibility and anxiety must have been a great strain on you. In such important transactions there is the ever present fear that the slightest slip or mistake may have such tremendous consequences and this is greatly increased when one is alone.

17 April 1885 (from G. Hughes, ex-commissioner)
    Just a line to heartily congratulate you on your great success in bringing the Franco-Chinese War to a conclusion on such favourable terms for the

latter country. It is indeed a great triumph for both the I.G. and yourself and will immensely enhance the value of the Customs Service in the eyes of Chinese and foreign residents in China to say nothing of the peoples of other lands. How Tseng, Li, and other Chinese diplomats in Europe will like it is another matter. Well done! You ought to get a handsome recognition for this clever business.

12 May 1885 (from Mr Archer Shee, ex-commissioner)

I cannot refrain from telling you what a sincere pleasure it has been to me to read of your brilliant and important success in the Public Affairs of France and China. It is of course a great source of satisfaction and pride to every one of his subordinates, present and past, to note the ever victorious march of their distinguished chief. Hitherto his great success— unchecked success—has been his own and only his own work. But on this occasion his efforts must have failed had there been only a slight want of tact and ability in his lieutenant. And indeed it seems to me that in this matter the only credit in the affair due to Sir Robert lies in the selection of his Ambassador.

8 July 1885 (from Sir W. Cairns)

I was very glad to see in this morning's Times that you had been created a C.M.G. Accept the sincere congratulations of an old friend. Do you succeed Sir Robert Hart as Chief of the Chinese Customs?

Canton, 15 July 1885 (from A. E. Hippisley)

I felt at times anxious as to whether you could stand such continual strain, for I could well see from the tone of your remarks what a very uphill game you had to fight. I trust the Chinese Government will give you some high decoration. I am sure you richly deserve it. I am only sorry you are not a Chinese scholar, for now that Sir Robert Hart has left us, you would be far and away the best man in the Service to succeed him . . . How on earth you did the work I am at a loss to understand.

In connection with these last letters it should be mentioned that almost simultaneously with the signing of the treaty Hart was offered, and at first accepted, the post of British minister in Peking. There were many speculations as to who would be his successor. Most people favoured Campbell, despite his long absence from China, which had naturally caused him to forget the language. Others thought to be in the running were James Hart (the I.G.'s brother),

Robert E. Bredon (the I.G.'s brother-in-law), and Gustav Detring. However, much to the relief of all, Hart changed his mind and in September 1885 wrote to Lord Salisbury asking him to accept his resignation as minister. There is no doubt that his decision was a relief to the Customs Service and to the Chinese (in particular to the Empress Dowager), who were all alarmed at the thought that the great I.G. might leave them. Campbell himself was delighted. "Well, the I.G. remains I.G.! Long life to him!" he wrote to a friend.

The Paris negotiations had brought Campbell into contact with many distinguished French statesmen, notably M. Ferry, M. Cogordan, and M. Billot, and the friendships thus contracted lasted. Never a New Year passed without some friendly letter, and M. Ferry in particular showed a warmth of affection which was quite remarkable. What I think chiefly attracted Ferry to Campbell was the latter's complete sincerity. It was also a gratification to Ferry to know that, in contrast to his own countrymen, who showed him a lack of appreciation for many years, Campbell loyally acknowledged the part he had played in the China treaty and recognised in him France's foremost statesman, which indeed he was. "Votre très affectionné," "Votre dévoué et affectionné," "Toujours à vous à coeur," are some of the ways in which Ferry ended his letters, and in a card written by him a few days before his death, when he was president of the Senate he wrote, "Bien touché de votre souvenir si fidèle et si affectueux." The letter of his that I like most was written on 4 May 1891, in reply to Campbell's congratulations on a great parliamentary success recently gained by him in the Vosges:

> Il m'est fort agréable de recevoir de temps en temps le témoignage de votre affectueux souvenir. Je ne cesse de féliciter de l'oeuvre à laquelle nous avons collaboré, que le temps consolide et justifie, et je constate avec grande satisfaction que depuis six années le gouvernement Chinois execute avec loyauté et sans aucune arrière pensée le traité de paix definitive dont nous avons été négociateurs.

M. Ferry, at any rate, was never backward, as were some others, including perhaps Hart himself, in acknowledging the supremely important part played by Campbell in the negotiations.

M. Billot, who afterwards became French ambassador at Lisbon and Rome, was also a regular correspondent. I will quote from only one letter. From Rome in January 1891 he wrote:

Votre billet affectueux m'a fait le plus vif plaisir. Je suis heureux de savoir que vous gardez un si bon souvenir de votre collaborateur de quelques mois. Soyez convaincu que je conserve aussi fidèlement les sentiments de sympathie et de haute estime que j'ai conçu pour vous en 1885.

M. Cogordan, who succeeded M. Billot as political director at the French Foreign Office and later proceeded to China on Campbell's advice to put the finishing touches to the treaty, remained his warm friend till his death in 1904. In February 1886, after his return from China, he wrote:

Je vous remercie—car je vous dois la mission que je viens de remplir. Il est bien certain que si vous n'avez donné l'idée de me faire envoyer en Chine pour y continuer l'oeuvre que nous avons commencé ensemble à Paris, cette idée ne me serait pas venue.

The Portuguese Treaty

During the whole of the anxious time in Paris Campbell had worked entirely alone, without any clerical staff to assist him, his only companion being his wife, who copied out for him in her own beautiful handwriting the numerous despatches and telegrams on which several thousands of pounds were spent. Indeed her handwriting subsequently became so well known to the Peking staff from her work in Paris that the treaty was often humorously referred to in Customs circles as Mrs Campbell's treaty. The responsibility and the strain had affected Campbell and when it was all over he was ordered by the doctors to recuperate at Smedley's Matlock. He had hoped to be spared other similar work in the future. Yet in eighteen months another opportunity came to him to display his diplomatic powers, and this time his task was the settlement of a treaty between Portugal and China.

As early as 1557 the Portuguese, in return, it is said, for ridding the China Sea of hordes of savage pirates, had been allowed to erect factories in Macao. Although the peninsula had long been in fact a colonial possession of Portugal, the Chinese government had persistently refused to recognise Portugal's sovereignty, alleging that she was merely a lessee. Indeed, until 1849 the Portuguese had actually paid a small annual rent. This diplomatic difficulty had prevented the conclusion of any commercial treaty, and a treaty had now become particularly desirable in connection with the opium traffic in this part of the world.

In December 1886 Campbell was sent to Lisbon to negotiate, and after four months of arduous work he succeeded in securing a protocol under which China confirmed perpetual occupation of Macao and its dependencies by Portugal, while Portugal undertook to cooperate in opium revenue work in the same way as Britain had recently undertaken to cooperate at Hong Kong. Portugal also engaged never to alienate Macao and its dependencies without the consent of China. Campbell was invested by imperial decree with full powers to sign the protocol on behalf of China, and the formal treaty was subsequently signed at Peking in April 1888. The negotiations at Lisbon were conducted by Campbell directly with Barros Gomez, Portuguese minister of foreign affairs, and his immediate subordinate Souza Roza. The latter subsequently proceeded to China, on Campbell's suggestion, to settle the final details.

Campbell seems to have found the negotiations very difficult. The following letter, written by him to my mother from Lisbon on 23 February 1887, shows that he was suffering from nervous strain:

I have played the last card and taken upon myself an immense responsibility as I did in Paris. Billot candidly acknowledged that if I had not acted as I did, the protocol would never have been signed; and he has said as much to the Ministers here. If, therefore, I pull the thing through, it will be by this supreme effort. If it succeeds, all well! If it fails, they will say here that they trusted to me, and that I am responsible for the failure. Again, if it succeeds the credit will go to somebody else, instead of myself as the "obscure negotiator." In Paris if I had acted according to the strict letter of my instructions instead of their spirit, the whole thing must have miscarried. So now! When one considers that I managed the whole Paris business by myself—keeping my own counsel—consulting nobody—without any staff to help me in my telegrams etc., and here also, being quite alone, and acting on my own judgment, it is almost more than one man can be expected to do . . . After the Paris negotiations, I hoped that I should never have anything of the kind to do again, and I say the same thing now. Although different in character, this negotiation has been even more difficult in some respects than the Paris one. The result must now be known in a day or two; and if it is favourable, I will send you a note which I want you to take to Sir Julian Pauncefote.

Campbell was apparently a little doubtful about letting Sir Julian Pauncefote know, for in another letter to my mother dated Lisbon, 6 March 1887, he said:

Sir Julian P. gave me a letter of introduction to M. Petre; but, as you know, after a few days experience of Lisbon, I decided that the best policy to follow was the one I adopted in Paris, namely to keep silent and inspire confidence by sincerity. As in Paris, so here, one of the chief difficulties has been to make them believe in Chinese sincerity as well as my own. I think I owe a return to Sir Julian for his kindness, and as the settlement of the Macao question is of such importance to Hongkong, I do not consider I am committing an indiscretion in letting him know that we are on the point of an agreement; because what remains to be done is simply a question of form or procedure—at least I hope so. I wish you therefore to take the enclosed letter to him, and say it does not require any reply, but I send it through you to make sure that it gets safely into his hands . . .

Then follows a characteristically humorous postscript:

On second thoughts, before taking the letter to Sir Julian, await a telegram from me. If I telegraph "Sun shines," take the letter to him and say that you have received a telegram from me, meaning that all is going well as I hoped—but if I telegraph "Rain falls," do not take the letter to him but keep it till I write or telegraph again.

Presumably the sun shone, for the protocol was signed shortly afterwards. Campbell was presented to the king of Portugal, who was very kind and complimentary and bestowed upon him the honour of Commander of the Order of Our Lady of the Conception of Villa Vicosa.

The protocol was not at first too well received by some of the Chinese. Mr Cartwright wrote from Tientsin after a visit to Li Hung-chang in June 1887:

I sat with the Viceroy for nearly 2 hours. He does not like the Macao settlement, thinking China has given too much. I put before him some considerations which, I think, made him view it in a different light. I am afraid M. Roza won't have an easy time of it in arranging the Treaty. Of course I told all this to the I.G. and he will use it as a lever to urge the Portuguese to give us the most active cooperation at Macao.

In November 1887 Cartwright wrote:

I think now Roza will get his Treaty. The principal difficulty is over the word "dependencies" in the Protocol. The Canton Viceroy is furious, and his position as Champion of the integrity of the Chinese dominions is such a strong one that it will not be easy to dislodge him. Detring is working on Li, who has recently reported that China cannot repudiate what was done at Lisbon. The Canton Viceroy would tear the Protocol up and fight.

All ended happily, however, for on 12 December Cartwright wrote:

> As you will have heard by telegram the Portuguese got their Treaty at the last moment. The difficulties have been adroitly turned, and Chang chi Tung has for the moment been jockeyed.

Arrangements were made in due course for the collection of duties in Macao by the Customs Service in the same way as in Hong Kong. The problem of collecting opium duties in China was not an easy one and Cartwright threw an interesting light on it in one of his letters to Campbell:

> The great difficulty has been to get out the old collectors. They die very hard, and are backed by the provincial authorities. The I.G. has his work cut out to establish the new order of things against the covert but very active opposition of the people, but he is very patient and dogged, and deals with each obstacle as it presents itself. I think we are assured of the loyal cooperation of the Hongkong Government, and Macao appears to be following suit. You will be pleased to hear that so far the Macao station has collected much more than the Hongkong station.

Campbell received some flattering notices in the press for this diplomatic success, and I quote the following from the *Times* of 11 April 1887:

> Paris, April 10. Mr Duncan Campbell, who, as will be remembered, materially contributed to bring about the treaty between France and China, has evidently a knack of overcoming the traditional slowness of Chinese diplomacy. For a quarter of a century China and Portugal had been discussing a treaty of friendship. Four months ago Mr Campbell started for Lisbon, and has just returned here, after concluding a treaty which will be promptly ratified, and will give China another ally in Europe. Portugal, as may be supposed, has conferred decorations on this expert negotiator, in sign of her satisfaction.

As with the French, so with the Portuguese statesmen, the friendships contracted during these negotiations survived, and many cordial letters from Barros Gomez and Souza Roza, afterwards Portuguese ambassador to the United States and to France, were amongst Campbell's papers. Here are extracts from two letters from Barros Gomez:

Lisbon, 3 July 1888

> J'espère que vous aurez reçu depuis longtemps un exemplaire du livre blanc sur les négociations avec la Chine . . . Croyez, mon cher Monsieur Campbell que je garderai toujours un bon souvenir de nos communs rapports, et de la façon loyale de traiter que vous avez toujours montré pendant les laborieuses négociations de Lisbonne.

78

Lisbon, 2 December 1891

Je reçois avec grand plaisir votre petit mot si amical et les voeux que vous formulez pour mon pays, moi et les miens. Dieu veuille que la nouvelle année nous apporte une entente entre le Portugal et l'Angleterre qui sauvegarde la dignité et les intérêts essentiels des deux pays. C'est là précisement un de mes voeux les plus ardents et les plus anxieux. Je garde toujours le meilleur souvenir des rapports que nous avons maintenu ensemble et de l'heureuse conclusion où nous avons abouté. Votre droiture d'esprit et loyauté de caractère y ont contribué puissamment.

Veuillez présenter mes respects a Madame Campbell et croyez moi toujours

Votre très devoué
Barros Gomez

The Lisbon treaty was the last in which Campbell was employed as negotiator. One other treaty fell to be managed by the Customs Service, namely that between China and India over the Tibet-Sikkim boundary; but it was arranged directly by Hart from Peking through the agency of his brother James, and Campbell does not appear to have been called upon to act, apart from some occasional interviews at the Foreign Office in London. The last reference I can find to Campbell as a diplomat is in 1903 when he apparently had some interviews with Marquis de Soveral, the Portuguese ambassador in London, over a new treaty between Portugal and China. He went to the marquis with the following letter of introduction from Souza Roza:

Légation de Portugal en France
Paris, 15 July 1903
Cher ami,

J'ai l'honneur de vous présenter Mr Duncan Campbell avec qui j'ai des relations très amicales depuis de longues années. Mr Campbell est l'ami de Sir Robert Hart et son délégué à Londres; c'est avec lui que j'ai commencé les négociations qui ont abouté au Protocole de Lisbonne lequel a servi de base au traité portugais-chinois de 1887. Ayant pu apprécier depuis lors la droiture de caractère et l'esprit d'équité de Mr Campbell je suis heureux de le mettre en rapport avec vous, sûr qu'il recevra la meilleure acceuil.

Mille amitiés de

Votre dévoué
Souza Roza

X

THE SINO-JAPANESE WAR, 1894-1895

Shortly before the outbreak of war between China and Japan over Korea in 1894, two great misfortunes befell Campbell. The first was the death of his eldest son, his "great hope" James Baillie Campbell, at Peking in September 1892. After a successful career at Cheltenham College, in which he had gained a great reputation as a cricketer, racquets player, and musician, Jim, as we called him, received from Sir Robert Hart a nomination to the Customs Service. And here let it be remarked that Hart knew how to do things gracefully. He timed the nomination so that it arrived on the recipient's birthday and he pleased the father by ending the official letter of appointment thus: "I am very glad to place this young gentleman's name on our Service List, and I trust that in the years to come he will have the opportunity of showing that he has inherited his father's power of doing good work well."

Jim was allowed as an act of grace to spend a few months in the London office to begin with, and during this time he was chosen to play cricket for the Gentlemen of Surrey under the captaincy of the famous Walter Read, who had formed a high opinion of his skill as a batsman. On proceeding to China early in 1892 Jim was at once attached to the Peking staff. Here he made himself popular all round by his charm of manner and by his exquisite violin playing. He was doing excellently when he was stricken by typhoid fever and died after a short illness less than a year after leaving England. On the night he died poor Campbell, who like many of our race was gifted with second sight, had a curious dream, in which his uncle Baillie—the old man who had acted as a father to him in his boyhood days—appeared before him and, pointing to a bed in which lay a stricken figure mortally ill, said, "There is blood, there is blood." Campbell was so impressed that he got out of bed, wrote down his dream, and put it into a sealed envelope. The following night a telegram arrived from Hart saying, "Much typhoid fever this autumn in Peking. Your son down with it and being devotedly nursed by Mrs Cartwright." Remembering his dream Campbell knew that this was merely a message preparing us for the worst. Hastily a telegram was despatched, "Love from all at home," but it was too late, for in a few hours another telegram arrived saying that all was over.

Campbell's hopes had been centered on his gifted first son, and he felt his death acutely. The depth of his grief is painfully evident in his replies to the numerous letters of sympathy. Yet he was man enough to think of those in China who had witnessed the death. In a letter to Mr Cartwright written in October 1892 he said: "I wrote to the I.G. that my first written words were to express my deep gratitude to all who had so affectionately attended our poor boy throughout his illness, especially Mrs Cartwright, and our sympathy for all the pain they must have felt. Will you kindly tell everybody the same thing." The first mail letters from China giving details of the illness and death, including three from Sir Robert Hart, alas never arrived, for they had gone down in the ill-fated *Bokhara,* wrecked off Formosa, and they were letters which of course could never be rewritten. But we heard later that the last thoughts of the sufferer were of his mother—"my darling mother," he kept repeating. The stricken parents sought consolation in Dean Farrar, who only a short time previously had lost a son in Peking, also in the Customs Service. The dean and Mrs Farrar kindly came over to Clanricarde Gardens to conduct a short memorial service in our drawing room. Later Campbell wrote pathetically to Mrs Farrar: "I suppose you know from Mrs Cartwright that, two or three days before he was taken ill, my son gathered a quantity of lovely red roses (his favourite flower), and placed them on the cross of your dear son's grave, and now the two boys lie side by side in the Peking cemetery." The letters of sympathy which Campbell perhaps valued most came from masters and boys at Cheltenham College. One of the masters who had been impressed by Jim's musical gifts wrote some charming In Memoriam verses which were afterwards printed and circulated. Another of the masters paid eloquent tribute to him in an obituary notice which appeared in the *Cheltonian.* It is too long to give *in extenso,* but I give the following extracts:

When alluding to his death in a sermon preached on the 9th October, Dr James said: "In him at least the life at school had not starved the artistic power, and those of us who can recall his playing at his last concert will not soon forget what to me at least seemed the touch of real genius which marked it. It is pleasant to remember that not long before he left England he went down to the Mission and used his gift to give

pleasure there to the people in the little Mission Room . . . He died on
Michaelmas Day. His body lay in the Chapel of the British Legation
during the night of the 30th, covered with flowers; and the Union Jack
was placed over the coffin by Sir John Walsham, the British Minister at
Peking. On the 1st October, his mother's birthday, he was laid to rest in
the English Cemetery, the prayers at the grave being read by Bishop
Scott. There was a very large attendance at the funeral, all the foreign
Legations being represented and all the flags were at half-mast . . . Bright,
cheerful, intelligent, good-tempered, high spirited, kind hearted, he made
friends wherever he went, and we at Cheltenham, the dear old school he
loved so well, about which he made constant inquiries in his letters home,
wish to bear testimony to the affectionate regard he inspired both in
masters and boys.

"Found faithful in very little" were the words Campbell had inscribed
over the tomb. Strange that in this pathetic way he should bequeath his own
humility to his son!

Campbell had barely recovered from this bereavement when a second
misfortune came upon him. He became heavily involved in the great Colman
and May smash and at one blow lost practically the whole of his private fortune. He bore his losses with extreme fortitude, but they weighed heavily on
his mind, and it was the thought of what he had lost for his family that
troubled him most on his death bed.

Then came another anxiety—China's war with Japan.

Korea was one of China's tributary states, and its Customs was under Sir
Robert Hart's indirect control. But Japan for centuries had had an interest in
the country. As far back as 1592 there had been a great military invasion by
Japan, and in more recent times war between China and Japan over Korea
had narrowly been averted in 1876 and again in 1882. In the latter year China
had sent troops to restore order, and these had been opposed by Japanese
troops. China, however, took a firm line, and Japan received a setback.
It was a question of sea power: China was closer to Korea's west coast. China,
thanks to the work done by Campbell and Admiral Lang, had a fine fleet, and
the opinion in naval circles was that Japan's fleet was hopelessly inferior to it.
Admiral Ting had gone to Korea with this fleet and (with Yüan Shih-k'ai) had
reinstated the Korean king and brought back to Tientsin as a prisoner the
king's usurping uncle (the Taiwongun), Japan's protégé. Friends of China were
jubilant.

In 1894 an insurrectionary movement broke out which led the Korean king, acting on the advice of Yüan Shih-k'ai, the imperial resident, to seek aid from China, which was duly sent. Japan also sent troops, refused to withdraw them, and declared war. China, for the reasons I have given in my earlier discussion of the Chinese fleet, no longer had the splendidly equipped fleet which had frustrated Japan's efforts twelve years before, and she was hopelessly unprepared. Japan on the other hand had long made ready, as Hart pointed out in the letter which I quote later. The Chinese Northern Fleet, which alone participated in the war (the Southern Fleet lay snugly in harbour all the time), went into action in the Yalu River battle with practically no ammunition on board. It had been hopelessly neglected since Admiral Lang's departure. The story is told that the flagship had only three live shells for its big guns, and it is said that of the shells fired the first missed, the second put the Japanese flagship out of action, and the third sank another Japanese ship. Then it was all over, and Admiral Ting, who managed to escape in his flagship to Weihaiwei, wrote a typical Chinese letter to the Japanese admiral and then committed suicide. It was a great blow to Campbell, who had done so much to create the Chinese fleet, to see all his labours wasted.

As the war went on, the Japanese, winning all along the line and their *amour propre* satisfied, wished to get out of the struggle gracefully, and there is evidence (a letter from Lady Hart to Campbell on 25 February 1895)** that in a roundabout way they tried to make this known to Hart. I can find nothing in Campbell's papers, however, which indicates that Hart himself took any active part in the peace negotiations. But Campbell was constantly in touch with the British Foreign Office during the latter part of the war and tried unsuccessfully to impress upon it the views held by Hart and himself as to the dangers to be anticipated in the East from Japan's success. Hart urged a treaty with China, and I quote from a remarkable letter he wrote to an English statesman in April 1895 shortly before the Treaty of Shimonoseki, negotiated by Li Hung-chang, ended the war. One can well imagine the shade of the great I.G. brooding over the disasters which have since overtaken the China he loved and served so long and well, and pointing, it may be, a finger of reproach at the statesmen of Europe who had neglected his advice and warning:

I can quite understand how all the world rejoices in Japan's success, for, emerging from the strictest seclusion only 3 decades back, that plucky nation has gone to work seriously, not by any means breaking entirely with the past, but ever going ahead of the leading Powers of the day in its prevision and preparation for the future.

China on the other hand has no sympathy: she has had opportunities and she has not improved them. She has rejected all sorts of advice and held on to her own ideas and she compares badly in the eyes of civilisation with her diminutive neighbour. The old saw puts "the proof of the pudding" in the eating," and, similarly the future will show whether the present has been wisely handled or mismanaged. European suspicions and jealousies and eventualities have tied the hands of the Treaty Powers, and nobody dares to do more than whisper some soft words of sympathy here, or give some friendly hint in favour of peace over there: China is very sore over what she considers the desertion of friends and Japan is really almost as sore over the good advice of the same amiable persons.

To my mind Europe has blundered and next century will see the East rolling the West back and, the mask off, paying off old scores in like coin! A few months ago the Japanese Press had nothing but good to say about England and took her for a model; a little later the tone altered and Japan began to pose as England's rival; still later evolution moved on further and the same Press began to inveigh against British policy and misdeeds and to sketch out for the future a crusade in which Japan, after settling Formosa, should proceed to restore Hongkong to "her" Chinese Empire and then free India's Princes from foreign tyranny. The War supplies abundant evidence that it had long been prepared for: China was carefully studied, and under the pretence of preparing to meet Russia and then of reforming Corea, armies were mustered and put into the field without the slightest cause for war other than what a scheme of conquest supplied. Every step was arranged in advance and every move carefully thought out—on the one hand crippling China and on the other craftily neutralizing Western Powers. Successful in both lines—fighting foreign diplomacy and China's myriads—she now begins to frame her serious programme, which is to lead the East in war, in commerce and in manufactures. Thus, hitherto England's customer, Japan henceforth will be England's rival and will strain every nerve to oust England and take her place, while China, pacific and not aggressive, is still undeveloped, doesn't want to compete, but, left to herself, will pass more and more under Japan's domination and finally help her game. We are now passing

84

out of the period when China, at bay, had to consider the best step to take: should she fight it out alone, taking the chance of extinction, and yet with final triumph not altogether impossible, or should she seek an ally, or should she submit? What a chance to thwart Japan and lead China! Properly managed China is an endless mine of wealth and power, and to nobody would she commit herself more readily and more trustingly than to England. But the chance is vanishing, for submission is almost determined on: the West will rue it and England more than the others, having lost possibilities that were, one might say, infinite. Some years ago certain leading Indian Buddhists visited Japan and ever since Japanese have been strolling through India, studying the Government, the people, the princes, aspirations, complaints, possibilities; time will develop the plot and the viper will then sting! The Japanese programme is a big one—bold, ambitious, and dangerous: no amiable talk, no friendly negotiation will divert her from her purpose, and this purpose will soon be seen at work, unless indeed the Russians, whose fleet has been increasing in these waters, take things in hand, interfere, and smash the wonderful mannikin. If I were a Japanese I should be proud beyond all expression of all that has been done, and I'd go in, heart and soul, for the fullest development: and I believe that is the feeling of every Japanese, man, woman and child. But, mind you, the stronger the feeling, the greater danger it covers for the future, for 30 years have not changed Japanese INNERNESS. The peace conditions will open all China—and all the world will applaud: but they will also force China to become a manufacturing country. They are also so craftily arranged that at any moment breach of treaty may be pleaded and further conquest effected, while they press so heavily on China that freedom of action is handicapped and the Govt so impoverished that despair rather than hopefulness will give the tone to everything that is attempted here.

My sorrow and anxiety have been pretty heavy the last 9 months and my work has been very fatiguing. I feel that the labour of reconstruction may fall on my shoulders. If I were 20 years younger, I'd go at it cheerily and perhaps make it a success, but now, over 60, and horribly fatigued by over 40 years constant work in China, I doubt if I can do more than give a little good advice, and whether that will be followed or whether this giant will just roll over to the other side and go asleep again, is still doubtful enough, for though beaten all along the fighting fringe, the heart of the country does not feel or acknowledge defeat yet. Japan, however, will stand no nonsense, and China will have to step out—but in whose interest will that be if the tune must be taken from Japan . . .

    P.S. Poor old Ting carried himself very well at Wei-hai-wei and the
calm way in which he wrote to Ito and then killed himself is very Chinese;
but we all blame him for not going out and sinking every transport
the morning they anchored in Yung Ching bay.

A truly remarkable letter this, and it seems almost incredible that anyone
could forecast so accurately such a long time ago events which have now
actually happened!

    The war over, China had to raise a loan to pay off the indemnity of
£30 million, and Campbell, acting on instructions from Hart, tried to get a loan
guaranteed by England. Owing mainly to the lethargy of the British government he was not at first successful, and Russia and France got the first loan
(£15,820,000) in July 1895. He and Hart continued to press the British Foreign Office, however, and here his old friend Lord James of Hereford was
useful in getting first George Curzon (afterwards Lord Curzon) and then Lord
Salisbury to listen to the strong representations made by Hart from Peking.
England was not too well served by her diplomats in the East at this time.
Cartwright wrote from Shanghai in August 1895, "I hope this new Russian
loan wont affect Hart's position. English influence out here has fallen almost
to zero, and I fear our present Minister is not the man to revive it." The
strange reluctance to follow Hart's advice puzzled others who knew the East.
Thus Sir Julian Pauncefote, writing to my father in 1897, says he "cannot
understand the obstacles that prevail in the face of advice from such a quarter."
Success did finally attend Hart's and Campbell's persistent efforts and England
(with Germany) got the second loan of £16 million.

    Li Hung-chang's reputation was greatly damaged by the failure of China's
armed forces during the war, and he must have had feelings of remorse for
having let Admiral Lang go. Moreover, he had tried to raise money for the war
by negotiating for a loan from a very shady financier in Paris. Mr Louis Rocher,
a French commissioner in the Customs Service, was in Paris at the time, and
there was some lengthy correspondence between him and Campbell, which
showed that these two did all they possibly could to warn the great viceroy of
the danger he was running. In 1896, the year after the war, Li went as China's
representative to the Czar's coronation; and afterwards he visited all the chief
European countries, as well as the United States. He was made much of and I
remember being present at a great dinner given in his honour in London.

Mr Hippisley, who was acting as Hart's right-hand man in Peking at this time, gave an interesting but gloomy picture of China as he then saw it in a letter to Campbell on 29 October 1896:

Li is back and appointed to the Yamen—but handed over to the Board on one and the same day for "straying into and inspecting the forbidden enclosure of Yuang-ming-Yuan." I believe he went with a large retinue of 70 or 80 persons, hence the trouble. China's only hope rests in him . . . I doubt, however, whether even Li will be able to galvanise this moribund empire. At present the one dominant idea seems to be that the Double Dragon decorations must be made less like baking dishes and more like Foreign Stars! What children they are, it is another case of Nero fiddling while Rome burns. Our own outlook appears to me to be pretty black. When the I.G. goes, as he will have to go some day (though I hope not yet), England will require an English successor, but Russia and France and possibly Germany also will fight for their own nominees; and with the enormous material pressure Russia can bring down on China, will England be able to carry her point? If she can't, then British trade is doomed. For though, as people say, the Customs procedure is established and has only to be followed, results depend more on the spirit in which rules are interpreted than on the rules themselves—and with a foreigner in command the interpretation would be anti-British: for all foreigners are puppets in the hands of their Governments. Look even at Detring— he has posed as being on bad terms with the Minister and now all German papers praise him for having always shown himself a thorough German and a true friend of German interests. Most of the others make no concealment of their national bias. I think therefore the I.G. makes a serious mistake in bringing von Grot back here.

What a curious case that is of Sun Wen. He is a nice little man, at least so he seemed to me some years ago at Macao, where at one time I saw a good deal of him.*

By the way can it be true—as is reported here—that Minister Kung never met Lord Salisbury till the latter's garden party to Li and that Li actually introduced him to the Premier and Foreign Secretary? Such a thing seems incredible.

---

*The reference here is presumably to Sun Yat-sen, who had been imprisoned in the Chinese Legation in London. Little was it thought at the time that he was destined to become the first president of the Chinese Republic! The British government was not too pleased with the part played by the Chinese minister and his English secretary, Sir Halliday Macartney, in the kidnapping of Sun Yat-sen, and this probably explains Lord Salisbury's reluctance to meet the minister.

XI

QUEEN VICTORIA'S DIAMOND JUBILEE

In 1897 came the Diamond Jubilee of Queen Victoria, and Campbell was appointed by imperial decree to act as secretary on the staff of the Chinese special ambassador, Chang Yin-huan. The Chinese minister in London, Lo Feng-luh, who was a friend of Li Hung-chang, had wished to act in this capacity but gracefully retired when he learned that it was the emperor's desire that Campbell should be made responsible. The special ambassador, who was the trusted friend and adviser of the emperor, was a dear old man, and he brought with him two handsome presents for Campbell, one of them a Chinese bowl of the Ming period, which is still in my possession. He also brought some imperial presents for Queen Victoria, which were forwarded under cover of the following letter drafted by Campbell:

> Your Majesty,
>
> Having been appointed by my August Sovereign to convey his congratulations for Your Majesty's prosperous reign of sixty years, I have now the honour to deliver to Your Majesty my letter of credence.
>
> The few presents from the Emperor of China and from Her Majesty the Empress Dowager are the expression of their Majesty's good will and sincere wish that Your Majesty may continue to reign prosperously and your life and health be prolonged.
>
> It will always be my continuous effort to promote and strengthen the friendly relations which so happily exist between the two countries.

The Chinese secretary was Liang Ch'eng (Liang Chen-tung), and he spoke English exceedingly well. The special embassy was a great success and the envoy was made a Knight Grand Cross of Saint Michael and Saint George, while Liang got a K.C.M.G. Campbell merely received the jubilee medal, but the Chinese government was more generous and bestowed on him the last, as it turned out, of his Chinese honours. The following appeared in the *London and China Telegraph* of 25 April 1898:

> In the last Chinese Customs Gazette we notice the following notification—"By Imperial Decree. On 21 November 1897 (Kuang Hsu, 23rd year, 10th month, 27th day) an Imperial Decree was received conferring the rank and honour set forth below in recognition of services rendered

when attached to the Jubilee Embassy of His Excellency the Special Ambassador, Chang Yin-huan:—J. D. Campbell, Commissioner, promoted to be First Class of the Second Division of the Imperial Order of the Double Dragon." In congratulating Mr Campbell on the bestowal of this new honour, we may note that the grade to which he now attains is equivalent to a Grand Cross of one of the British Orders.

Chang Yin-huan, on returning to China, became the young emperor's right-hand man in the reform movement of 1898. Decree after decree was issued ordering such things as the abolition of the examination system, the founding of colleges and high schools in the provinces, the publication of official gazettes all over the empire, the institution of naval colleges, the establishment of railway and mining bureaus, the abolition of outmoded and useless government offices and sinecures. It seemed as if at last China was going full steam ahead. But for a conservative nation like China all this was too fast, and it was a misfortune for the young emperor that Prince Kung, the oldest and ablest of the imperial princes, died just before the reform movement started, and there was no one left on the emperor's staff to advise greater moderation. The result is well known.

The old Empress Dowager, who had been keeping a close watch on all these developments and whose life now seemed threatened, came out of her retirement and, with the backing of the army, made the emperor a prisoner. Chang Yin-huan, who had taken an active part in the movement, was also imprisoned and would have been executed but for the intervention of the British minister. As it was, he was sentenced to banishment and eventually executed by order of the cruel Prince Tuan at the beginning of the Boxer movement. Sir Liang Ch'eng had been careful not to become involved and was more fortunate. He was appointed Chinese secretary to the special envoy who was sent to attend King Edward's coronation in 1902, and later became Chinese minister at Washington. He maintained close and friendly relations with Campbell to the end and frequently wrote to him.

XII

RAILWAYS, POSTAL SERVICE, AND MINING

Writing from Peking in July 1867, Campbell had said, "The three things required of the Chinese are railways and telegraphs, audience with the Emperor, and Embassies." All these duly arrived in Campbell's time, though some of them were long in coming. Thus, the first embassy to Europe was despatched in 1876, but it was not until 1891 that formal audience was granted by the emperor, largely through the influence of Marquis Tseng. Hart thought the events of sufficient importance to wire Campbell giving some details, and his telegram is quoted in a letter of 6 March 1891 from Campbell to James Hart: "There were 6 Ministers, 4 Chargés d'Affaires with Secretaries, Attachés and Interpreters, some 30 in all present at the Audience."

A telegraph system which linked Peking with Europe was in full operation by the early seventies, and by means of it Hart and Campbell kept in the closest touch. Telegrams were constantly passing between them, and they had a three-letter cipher of their own, to the use of which they became so habituated that they could usually decipher the message straightaway without consulting the code. The cipher was of course kept under lock and key and was the despair of those who might seek to unravel its secret.

The Chinese had at first been violently opposed to the telegraph and the story of their conversion is amusingly told in H. A. Giles's book on the civilisation of China. A wily Cantonese had learned by telegram the names of the three highest graduates in the Peking examination some weeks before the news could reach Canton by the usual route, and he made a pot of money by buying up the lottery tickets bearing their names (lotteries were always held in connection with these examinations). Chinese opposition promptly collapsed like a pack of cards!*

Railways were a long time in coming, the Chinese showing a reluctance to entrust their management and finance to foreigners and at first idly conceiving that they could manage them by themselves. And when, after the

---

*Herbert Allen Giles, *The Civilization of China* (London, Williams and Norgate, 1911), p. 126.

Japanese war, they tackled the problem in earnest with the aid of foreign loans and concessions, they made the mistake of not employing the Customs Service, the one able administrative body in China, to manage the business for them. As Mr Cartwright said in a letter to Campbell in July 1895, "The Government should create a special Department for Railways and place it under the I. G. He could easily provide the greater part of the staff from the Service." As it was, there was endless muddle and maladministration, and many a quarrel among foreigners, resulting from conflicting claims and concessions.

Although the Customs Service was never directly concerned with China's railway schemes, the Campbell correspondence throws interesting sidelights on some of the earlier railway ventures. A pioneer railway connecting Shanghai with Wusung was started with foreign capital in 1875. But no regular permission had been obtained from the Chinese government, and after it had been running for about eighteen months it was purchased by the Chinese authorities and thereupon came to a speedy end. To quote from a letter written by Mr Cartwright from Peking in November 1876, "It was a conspicuous example of how not to do things." Cartwright's prophecy that after its purchase all traffic would cease and that the rails would probably be moved to Formosa to serve as tramways for the coal mines there turned out to be absolutely correct. After this fiasco, vain attempts were made from time to time by the Chinese themselves to start a few railways. Thus in 1888 a line was built on Li Hung-chang's initiative to connect Tientsin with the coal mines at Kaiping, a distance of some eighty miles. The intention had been to extend this line ultimately as far as Port Arthur, and had this project materialised it would undoubtedly have been a great advantage to China in her war against Japan. But nothing was done for several years. It is extraordinary to think that this short line was the only railway China had before 1895.

In 1889 again Li Hung-chang proposed building a line to connect Tungchow, a village on the Peiho close to Peking, with Tientsin and thus place the capital in communication with the coast. But this fell through, as did a rival project, proposed by the fire-eating viceroy Chang Chih-tung, to build a strategic line from Peking to Hankow. Both proposals were referred to in Cartwright's letters to Campbell of this year.** On the latter project he remarked: "This is the line Chang chi Tung recommends in opposition to Li's

Tientsin-Tungchow line, and he has been sent to Hankow to carry out his ideas which are to allow foreigners as little to do as possible with the construction of the line. Native capital, native talent and native materials are to be employed as far as possible so that all the profits may be kept for the Chinese. As not a single Chinaman will subscribe a dollar unless the management is placed in foreign hands, the chances of enjoying a run to Hankow by rail at an early date are not great!" Cartwright's prophecy was correct, as usual, for the line was not completed until 1907.

It was not till after the war with Japan that the railway problem was tackled seriously, with the aid of foreign loans and concessions, China having at last recognised that she was incompetent to do the business herself. Many of the loans were arranged by the Hong Kong and Shanghai Bank in London, and since they were secured on the Customs revenue Campbell was naturally in constant communication with the bank. Apart from this the Customs Service, unfortunately for China, had little to do with railway construction and administration. Nor was it much concerned with the later developments which took place after Campbell's death.

In the establishment of a postal system, on the other hand, the Customs Service took a leading part. The Service had had from its early years a courier postal service of its own, the Tsungli Yamen having delegated to Customs responsibility for collecting and delivering mails for the various foreign legations in Peking. Mail was carried by mounted couriers between Peking and Shanghai via Tientsin, except in the winter months when Tientsin was ice-locked and an overland route was used between Peking and Chinkiang, via Tientsin. In 1878 Hart instructed Detring, who was then commissioner at Tientsin, and who had organized the winter overland service in 1876, to experiment with an expansion of the postal service. The service between Tientsin and Peking, which had been running several times a week, began a daily run. Postal departments were created at the customhouses in several additional ports, with a view to further expansion. In 1878 also the Customs post for the first time issued its own stamps. Finally, late in 1878 the Customs postal facilities were made available to the general public.

Detring and Henry Kopsch, who was commissioner in Chinkiang and responsible for legation mails there, and who subsequently became a leading advocate of a national postal system for China and China's first postal secretary (in 1896), were responsible for the expansion attempt. Campbell was also consulted because of his past experience as an official in the postmaster general's office in England. Detring and Kopsch, enthusiastic but insufficiently experienced, were rather inclined to rush matters and there was a battle royal between Detring and Campbell over the stamps. Detring wanted stamps of his own design, which he said the I. G. had approved, and was annoyed when Campbell refused point-blank to carry out his instructions without definite authority from Hart. Campbell also obtained the best professional advice about stamps, which ran counter to Detring's proposals. More than once he had to write to Detring urging caution: "Without proper appliances it would simply be courting imperfection," he wrote to him in August 1877. But Detring was an obstinate man who liked to have his own way, and, relying on his close friendship with Li Hung-chang, he felt strong enough to flout at times even Hart himself.

In March 1879 Campbell wrote to Cartwright: "From the accounts in the newspapers the postal experiment seems to have been a failure. It is a pity to commence a service of that kind before the arrangements have been properly matured. The stamps are a most crude affair and do not possess any of the qualities requisite for a true stamp." Subsequently I find the following in a letter written by F. E. Taylor to Campbell from Peking in June 1881: "When passing through Tientsin I had tiffen with the Detrings. I had a long talk with Detring . . . on the postal stamp business. I explained that your anxiety on the matter and your wish to have the postal service securely instituted had been the cause of your not fulfilling his requisition, and of course you had no authority from the I. G. I also said that you were authorised by the I. G. to obtain professional advice in the matter, and that professional advice was strongly against the matter being started in the proposed way. He said he preferred the design he sent to those submitted by de la Rue!! He told me he does everything for Li through agents, who get their 5% and save all bother about getting authority from the I. G. and so on."

It was not until 1896, after the Japanese war, when railways, on which an efficient postal service must necessarily depend, were rapidly being constructed, that an imperial postage system was at last securely established. Hart was made responsible for it and became postmaster general, in addition to his other duties. In its formation Campbell played his usual active part behind the scenes, and when all was completed he was nominated by the Tsungli Yamen as China's delegate in Europe for all postal matters, his appointment being duly made known to all countries forming the Postal Union. This new duty took him occasionally to Berne to attend the meetings of the Postal Union as China's representative.

Under Customs supervision the new postal service was excellently run, and a fresh fruitful source of revenue was opened up for the imperial exchequer.

It remains to say a few words about mining activities. It may come as a surprise to many people to learn that at one time the Customs Service took an active part in the development of China's mining industry. China is exceedingly rich in coal fields and there were mines which had been worked by natives on and off for centuries. In 1874 the government suddenly decided to develop the industry and to introduce modern appliances. Campbell was instructed to make inquiries about suitable mining engineers who could proceed to China to examine the coal fields. After careful inquiries he made his selection, one of the appointments being that of Mr D. Tyzack.

The mines in Formosa were the first to be exploited, and the commissioner employed to superintend the scheme was Herbert E. Hobson. All went satisfactorily and in October 1875 Campbell sent a congratulatory letter to Hobson in which he said, "I congratulate you sincerely on the success that has crowned your efforts to induce the Authorities to work the coal mines at Keelung, and from the fact that Mr Tyzack is coming home to select men and material I congratulate myself on having selected a man in whom you appear to have such confidence." The Chinese government appears to have been pleased with the progress made, for in the following year Hart sent a telegram saying that he had been authorised to employ another mining engineer and shaft sinkers for the Hupei mines, and he gleefully ended his wire: "Chinese Authorities begin to come more to Customs for advice. They see our Service contains people of character and understanding." How long the Customs continued to do this kind of work for China I am not clear, but it must have been a sad blow when Formosa, with its mines, had to be surrendered to Japan in 1895.

XIII

THE BOXER RISING, 1900

At the beginning of 1900 the so-called Boxer Rising broke out. The old Empress Dowager sympathised with the movement; after many fluctuations, she had at last been induced by the extremists to believe that the only way of preserving the dynasty was to wipe out all foreigners. There was some excuse. China indeed had received provocation enough in recent years and was now completely maddened by the un-Christian conduct of the so-called Christian nations of Europe who, one after another, had taken advantage of her military weakness to seize, on the most slender pretexts, portions of her territory. Germany had started the ball rolling in 1897 by occupying Kiaochow, Russia had followed by occupying Port Arthur, and Great Britain in self-defence had felt constrained to obtain a long lease of Weihaiwei. The ignorant zeal of some of the Christian missionaries had further embittered China, and to many Chinese it appeared outrageous that efforts should be made to force upon their countrymen a religion whose followers, far from practising the Christian morality, had behaved little better than pirates and robbers. The Chinese, when left to themselves, have been the most peaceful of men, and the violence and cruelty shown by them during this rising can only be explained by the intensity of the provocation they had received.

By June 1900 Peking was completely cut off and the news got abroad that all the Europeans, including Sir Robert Hart and his staff, had been massacred. Lord Salisbury, fearing the worst, sent for Campbell and asked him to be ready at a moment's notice to go out to China to take Hart's place. Campbell pleaded that his age and his long absence from China, during which he had almost completely forgotten the language, rendered him unsuitable, and he appears to have suggested that Mr Hippisley should be asked to act instead. There are some curious notes among his papers, written in an unknown hand and enclosed in an envelope marked "Hippisley and the F. O.," which advance strong reasons why F. E. Taylor, the statistical secretary, then resident in Shanghai, who was apparently the nominee of the consular body, should not be chosen, and in the end Campbell's advice was followed and the Foreign Office decided to support Mr Hippisley.

Meanwhile the *Times* of 17 July 1900, believing that the worst had happened, published a long obituary notice of Hart, and Dean Gregory made arrangements for a memorial service at Saint Paul's. All through this anxious time Campbell had been despatching a constant stream of telegrams to the commissioners at the various ports asking for information, in particular to Paul King, who was in close touch with Li Hung-chang at Canton. He could obtain nothing definite but persisted nevertheless in the belief that Hart was still alive. As soon, therefore, as he heard of Dean Gregory's proposal to hold a memorial service he hastened to Saint Paul's and asked the dean to countermand or at any rate to postpone the service. His interview with the dean was stormy and unsuccessful. "Oh, I suppose you have come for a ticket," began the dean. "No," replied Campbell, "I have come to ask you to cancel the service. I don't believe Sir Robert Hart is dead. There is still hope." "That is impossible," said the dean, "everything has now been arranged, and things have gone too far." "Well," said Campbell, "all I can say is that I consider your action deplorable, and I must now make representations elsewhere." He accordingly proceeded to the Foreign Office and saw Lord Salisbury.

The latter agreed that the memorial service was at least premature; he could not actually prohibit it, but he would at any rate let it be known that the service had not the sanction of the government. His secretary accordingly wrote to Campbell on 20 July, "Lord Salisbury did not think we could do more than inform the Press that the proposal to hold a service for those who are supposed to have perished at Peking did not emanate from Her Majesty's Government. This has been done." Campbell at the same time got his friend Spenser Wilkinson of the *Morning Post* to write an appropriate leading article in that paper. Dean Gregory, now thoroughly alarmed, had to capitulate, and thus was prevented what would have been a deplorable fiasco. For sure enough, a few days later arrived the news that Sir Robert Hart was safe. It was rather characteristic of Hart that the first news as to his safety was gathered from a telegram ordering a new suit of clothes from Poole's, his tailor in Savile Row!

Paul King* gives a full account of the episode from the China end and refers to the numerous telegrams from the London office asking himself and others for news and suggesting Li Hung-chang, with whom King was then

*King, chap. 12.

in close touch, should be invited to cooperate. The great viceroy, whose anxiety was extreme, took this request from Campbell as a compliment and certainly did his best to obtain news and to prevent the tragedy of a massacre, and in this he was strongly supported by Prince Ch'ing, the senior of the Manchu princes, who had strongly resisted the movement from the first and had refused to let his troops take any part in the attack on the legations.

Hart, who had behaved heroically throughout the siege (even his worst enemies admitted that), when all was over wrote a series of articles for the *Fortnightly*. It was his first literary effort for the public and he was a little doubtful as to the prudence of publishing. He wrote to Campbell in September 1900: "Did you get my pencilled paper on the Legations? I wonder did the Fortnightly think it worth publishing. I also wonder if I was prudent in publishing it? . . . I cannot enrich literature but I think I can produce a train of thought which will not occur to another." The gist of the articles was that if the powers continued to treat China as in the past, China would arm her countless millions and, peaceful nation though she was, would ultimately seek her revenge for all the injuries she had suffered. He strongly urged that the powers cease to treat China as a nation of inferior civilisation (which was far from being the truth) and henceforward regard her as an equal. It was a Christian appeal to Christian nations, and I cannot refrain from quoting the following panegyric on the Chinese, written by a man who knew them better than any other European either before or since:

> They are well-behaved, law-abiding, intelligent, economical and industrious; they can learn anything and do anything; they are punctiliously polite, they worship talent, and they believe in right so firmly that they scorn to think it requires to be supported or enforced by might; they delight in literature, and everywhere they have their literary clubs and coteries for learning and discussing each other's essays and verses; they possess and practice an admirable system of ethics, and they are generous, charitable and fond of good works; they never forget a favour, they make rich return for any kindness, and, though they know money will buy service, a man must be more than wealthy to win public esteem and respect; they are practical, teachable and wonderfully gifted with common-sense; they are excellent artisans, reliable workmen, and of a good faith that everyone acknowledges and admires in their commercial dealings; in no country that is or was has the commandment "Honour thy father and Mother" been so religiously obeyed,

or so fully and without exception given effect to, and it is in fact the key-note of their family, social, official and national life, and because it is so "their days are long in the land God has given them."

The *Letters of John Chinaman* written about this time by (as it afterwards was revealed) a famous Cambridge don, went even further than Hart's articles in condemning the treatment of China. Much to the chagrin of Lady Hart, who was of a mercenary turn of mind, Hart never took a penny for his articles; a cheque for seventy-five pounds for the first of them was returned by Campbell to the publishers, Chapman and Hall. The articles were subsequently incorporated into a book entitled *These from the Land of Sinim*. The title chosen for the book and the mode of choosing were characteristic of Hart. When Campbell asked him what he would like the book to be called, the great man's reply was a telegram which merely cited Isaiah 49:12. Campbell was a bit puzzled and it was not until he had the telegram repeated that he realised that the last few words of verse 12 were intended. It is told of Hart that he read his Bible regularly from beginning to end each year, and this little incident certainly affords some corroboration.

The peace protocol was signed at Peking on 7 September 1901, the Chinese plenipotentiatries being Prince Ch'ing and Li Hung-chang; only two months later Li died brokenhearted and exhausted. The matter of indemnity remained for settlement, and it was not an easy matter to bring the powers into agreement on this complicated subject. Ultimately it was decided to exact an indemnity of 450 million taels and it was left to Hart to devise a plan for paying it off. In an envelope marked "confidential" I found copies of a number of telegrams which passed between Hart and Campbell in May 1901 and also notes of interviews with the Foreign Office and with Rothschild. Hart's plan was finally adopted.

During the time Hart was locked up in Peking, Paul King had been asked to act as a kind of I. G. for the southern ports, and the consular body had asked F. E. Taylor, the statistical secretary, to deputise at Shanghai. These two men did their best in difficult circumstances, but Hart, on again assuming power, was not too pleased with them and was in particular annoyed with Taylor's activities. But as Taylor explained in an indignant letter which he wrote to Campbell,** the situation had been exceedingly awkward and he had done what he had thought to be his duty.

Hart's house and all his belongings, the acquisition of a lifetime, were destroyed during the siege, and an insolent attempt by the Italian minister, Marquis Salvago, to appropriate the land on which Hart's house had stood led to Campbell's visiting Rome in the summer of 1901 to put the matter right. The Italian government was at first unreasonable, but in the end the matter was satisfactorily settled and Hart's new house was erected on the foundations of the old. It so happens that Campbell kept among his papers a copy of the letter he wrote to Hart on these Roman negotiations, and it is worth quoting as showing his diplomatic tact. Madame di Luca, an Italian lady of some influence and personally known to Sir Robert, placed herself at Campbell's disposal and was of some help. Writing to Sir Robert after the event she said, "Mr Campbell conducted the business with great tact and prudence, and made a most favourable impression at the Foreign Office . . . He is, as you know, beyond praise; it is rare to meet with a character so upright, thorough and conscientious, and quite refreshing to come in contact with what is now banished from this world of intrigue." Here are some portions of Campbell's letter:

Z. 1280   Rome, 19 July 1901

My dear Sir Robert,

Here we have been since the 1st instant, waiting patiently for Marquis Salvago's Report . . . Perhaps it is as well that the F. O. has heard your statement of fact before receiving the Minister's report and forming a preconceived idea.

Mr Buchanan [the British chargé in Rome] read me the telegram he sent to the F. O. after our interview with M. Prinetti [the Italian minister of foreign affairs], also the one sent on by the F. O. to Sir E. Satow [the British minister in Peking], whilst I showed him those I had sent to you.—They will have given you a fair idea of the state of feeling here.

Anticipating some reference to the telegrams etc. appearing in the Times last February, I telegraphed to you inquiring how far Reuter's telegram of 23 Feb. represented your protest, but I was not prepared for the outburst of indignation on the part of M. Prinetti who declared the Times articles were an outrage and an insult to his Govt and that Dr Morrison's telegrams [Morrison was the *Times* correspondent in Peking] had been inspired by you. Upon my remonstrating and asserting that it was a mistake to suppose such was the case, he repeated that they had certainly been inspired by you as you were known to be

Dr Morrison's most intimate friend. I observed that, although you were no doubt on friendly terms of acquaintance with Dr Morrison, I had reason to believe that you were not on such intimate terms of friendship as he had been led to suppose, and that some of Dr Morrison's telegrams had been the reverse of favourable to yourself, whilst the Times itself had been occasionally unpleasant. But how, remarked M. Prinetti, could he get such information except through you! I replied that it was probably the current talk of the place "les bruits qui couvraient sur place" but that Dr Morrison had the means of obtaining information at Peking such as none of the Ministers had. Mr Buchanan quietly put in "The Times often does a lot of harm." M. Prinetti responded to the effect that we might think him rather hard (un peu dur) but he had not words to express the anger and annoyance he felt upon seeing the accusation against Italy in the Times.—Then Mr Buchanan's turn came:—After stating that it would be gratifying to H. M.'s Govt if the Italian Govt could, without prejudice to its interests, restore this land to you, he referred to the great services you had rendered to all nations having commercial relations with China. M. Prinetti exclaimed "pas a nous," adding in a somewhat bitter tone that you had not been agreeable to the Italian Govt. Mr Buchanan did not ask him in what manner, but I interposed with the observation that you had always done what you possibly could to facilitate and promote commercial intercourse between foreign nations and China, and had thereby earned the thanks of various Governments. "At any rate, Sir Robert Hart has not been agreeable to us, far from it," M. Prinetti repeated more than once; but, at the same time, he said he had no wish to be disagreeable to Sir Robert Hart, if he had no reason to be agreeable to him. M. Prinetti calmed down during the remainder of the interview, but I only describe these two incidents here, leaving the rest for my official report . . .

I saw Mr Buchanan at the Embassy on Monday the 15th upon arriving from his country residence, and showed him a note I proposed sending M. Prinetti if he agreed with me it would be proper to do so, seeing that we are working together. He thought it would be well to send it as it was polite and dignified, but he advised my omitting "one way or the other" at the end of your telegram, as it might lead M. Prinetti to suppose that you did not mind what the decision might be. I enclose copy of the letter.

Mr Buchanan has been very kind . . . Madame di Luca, too, has been very kind. It appears that when she first heard of the Italian occupation of your ground, she went to M. Malvano (with whom she is on friendly and visiting terms) and pointed out what a mistake it was. After learning from me what the present state of things is, she went and saw M. Malvano privately of her own accord, taking with her the Decennial Reports, the Service List and some of the Customs publications which her son had sent to her—to show him the magnitude and importance of the Service and the estimation in which you are held by the several foreign Powers etc, etc. She said she had told him several plain truths, and I only hope she did not go too far, as she is evidently a clever and pushing woman and does not seem to mind what she says. According to her statement, they are absolutely ignorant at the [Italian] F. O. of the status of the Chinese Customs Service, and associate its duties with those of the Douanes in European countries, where it is looked down upon as the lowest of the Govt Departments. She had frequently, she said, heard people say that the Service ought to be known to the world by some other designation which would confer upon it the recognition which it deserves—the titles also of Inspector (Inspecteur) and Commissioner (Commissaire) being quite infra dig.!

I telegraphed to Bruce [Hart's son, in the London office] that if the Italian F. O. is not on our list, to send me the latest Customs publications and they are being sent by post c/o British Embassy. I have prepared a short Memo explanatory of the origin and scope of the Inspectorate General etc., which Mr Buchanan considers very interesting, in case there may be a favourable opportunity to present it with the Yellow Books to M. Malvano . . .

The Italians are just like the Portuguese—one has to humour them and rub their backs the right way. I allowed M. Prinetti to let off steam without interrupting him. I assented to whatever seemed reasonable, such as his inability to discuss the question until he had Marquis Salvago's report sous les yeux. I thanked him for his bon acceuil, and I think I left a good impression.

Hart bore the loss of his possessions like the philosopher he was, but he felt acutely the failure of the Empress Dowager to protect his person, and here is an interesting letter which he wrote to Campbell on 1 November 1900. (I should explain, by the way, that he had been in the habit of making an annual gift of the imperial tea to Queen Victoria, who drank none other.)

Kindly write a note to the Queen's Secretary and explain that just as the time came last June for ordering the usual supply of tea for Her Majesty's use, the Boxers upset all city arrangements and I could neither send it off nor procure it. I was specially sorry to have to take refuge in the Legation with this undone, but it gives me the chance to certify that dictionaries would be wrong to exclude the word "impossible"! The whole street where my teamen lived was burnt: do you remember it—the fine broad street running north from the How-men to the Bell Tower north of the Maishan or Coal Hill, with rich shops gaily decorated with all sorts and hues of fantastic wood carving on both sides? Once so busy, rich and prosperous—you can't imagine what a scene it now is of destruction and desolation! The Empress Dowager's attempt to wipe us out and the Boxer Crowd's atrocities, followed up by the cruel doings of all who had scores to pay off where well-to-do Chinese were concerned, have hit this quaint capital a blow it will not recover from for generations. My own neighbourhood and my own house were in the thick of it all, and it is just heartbreaking to stroll through it now and carry about the consciousness of having lost all the treasured souvenirs of half a century. The afternoon we fled to the Legation—while I went to the south bridge to look round, Hubert James went to the north: he was shot there, but I came back safe—it was a mere toss up that I did not go north instead of south. People blame me for staying on here, but I dont like to leave the ship while on her beam ends: let's right her first!

The Italian business satisfactorily settled, Hart set about building a new house on the foundations of the old and it was not long before he was re-established there. A letter to Campbell from Paul King in July 1904** gave a pleasing description of him in his new quarters and also described Peking after the siege. Here is an extract from that letter:

I am very glad to say that Sir Robert struck me as being in very good case. He seemed younger and stronger than he was in 1899, and has apparently suffered no ill effects from the siege. He kindly asked us to lunch and was very cheerful and pleasant. He did not mention many people by name but he made many inquiries about you and yours, not forgetting the little grandson. The old house has been restored on its former lines, as happily the original foundations were left intact by the Boxers, though they burnt the walls down; and he has re-established himself in precisely the old way. He talks of giving up in a few months, but I should think he will do nothing of the kind as he is really a wonderful man and seems to carry his great load of work and worry quite easily. In fact he looks considerably more vital than his staff, as both Piry and Aglen seemed rather fagged to my fancy.

I was interested to see the scene of the siege, I simply cannot imagine how a soul escaped to tell the tale. They were certainly encompassed on every side. Now the place is all altered, and a big foreign quarter has been laid out between the Chien Men and the Ha Ta Men, with the Chinese all cleared away. The railway runs right up to the Chien Men, through the outer wall, and a certain unique charm has departed from the city. There is far less crowd, and the natives seem quite cowed. They have not the spirit to insult us now . . .

XIV

THE CHINESE SPECIAL ENVOY AT KING EDWARD'S CORONATION

Anxious to ingratiate herself with England after the Boxer Rising, China sent a prince of the royal blood to attend King Edward's coronation in 1902. The prince chosen was His Imperial Highness Prince Tsai Chen, the eldest son of Prince Ch'ing, who since the death of Li Hung-chang had become the foremost man in China. He had strongly opposed the Boxer Rising and was in consequence *persona grata* with the powers. It was regarded as a great compliment to Campbell that Prince Ch'ing should have specially asked that he be made the secretary of the special embassy. With the Prince came Sir Liang Ch'eng, K.C.M.G., who had previously attended Queen Victoria's Diamond Jubilee, and a numerous suite. But the prince never attended the ceremony after all, for towards the end of June the king fell ill and everything had to be postponed.

I remember that on the day on which the coronation was to have taken place, I was given the privilege of escorting the prince by special train to Oxford. I made all arrangements the day before with Dr Strong, the dean of my old college, Christ Church, and the dean received him in state. The prince arrived in full paraphernalia, peacock feather and all, drove around Christ Church Meadows, visited New College and Magdalen, and charmed the heads of colleges, who had been invited to meet him at luncheon at the Deanery, by his dignified and courteous bearing. The only contretemps occurred at Magdalen, where Dr Warren rather rudely kept him waiting till he had finished addressing a meeting of the Magdalen tenants.

The prince, on my father's advice, refused several invitations from public bodies to attend various functions, and his delicacy of feeling during this time of national anxiety was much appreciated. In particular the following letter written by Campbell to the Lord Mayor of Manchester was widely circulated and approved:

Hotel Cecil, London, June 26, 1902
My Lord Mayor,

I am directed by His Imperial Highness, Prince Chen, to convey to you his high appreciation of the kind and hospitable invitation from the Corporation of Manchester.

His Highness feels that, whilst the nation is full of grief and anxiety, it would be better that he should sacrifice his own wishes and give up for the present the pleasure which he had anticipated in visiting your city.

His Highness is prolonging his stay until Monday next in hope that the encouraging reports of the King's progress will be maintained; and, if all is well, he proposes, after visiting Belgium and France, to return to England on his way to America, and then, if possible, to pay a short visit to Manchester.

Before leaving England, the prince presented Campbell with two magnificent cloisonné vases, very old and much finer than any I have seen at the British Museum or elsewhere. He also honoured him by attending a truly regal dinner which Campbell gave him and his suite at Clanricarde Gardens.

Campbell was given special leave by the king to wear his Chinese Order of the Double Dragon at court during the coronation ceremonies, but it was not till 1905 that King Edward granted him permission by licence under the Sign Manual to wear the order permanently.

XV

CAMPBELL'S CLOSING YEARS, 1903-1907

The problems deriving from the Boxer Rising having been settled, business at the London office resumed normal lines and became less exacting. Campbell at last found time to devote his attention to the preparation of a pension scheme for the Service, a matter which had long been in his mind. He prepared a draft scheme, which he submitted to counsel for their opinion on the legal aspects, and in due course the finished scheme was sent to Peking. Hart, however, shelved the whole matter and decided that it should be left to his successor. He may possibly have thought that the existing scheme, his own creation, under which, after every seven years, one year's full extra pay was given to every member of the Service, was generous enough. Generous it certainly was, but its weakness was that there was no certainty that the extra pay would be treated as capital and wisely invested.

Meanwhile in China reform was in the air, and in May of 1906 an edict was issued creating all sorts of new government boards, under one of which, the Shui-wu ch'u, the Customs Service was placed. Much perturbation was felt; a letter from Hippisley to Campbell** shows what anxiety was felt in the Service. Questions were asked in Parliament. Hart's own position does not appear to have been much affected, however, and the Chinese trusted him as much as ever. But people had begun to wonder what would happen when he left, and the question of his successor was becoming troublesome. Hart himself was in favour of Sir Robert Bredon, his brother-in-law, but Bredon was not *persona grata* with either the Service or the British Foreign Office, and when Hart asked Campbell to try and find out the Foreign Office's reasons, the latter found it difficult to reply. I have come across the draft of a letter Campbell wrote to Hart in May 1903. The draft is scored through and through, showing how uneasy Campbell felt at having to criticise his old friend Bredon, and it is not easy to say what exactly he wrote in the end. The best I can make of his draft is this:

London, May 1st, 1903

I enclose translations of the three telegrams I sent you on April 18, 19, and 21 and the one I received from you on 19 April.

I was thinking how I could best set about getting some reliable information outside the F. O., when the Globe Article of 17 April afforded me an excuse for making the inquiry I did. The person to whom I showed it remarked that Bredon would never be I. G., and when I asked "why so" seemed rather surprised that I should put the question and replied "I can simply tell you in the strictest confidence that the Govt will neither recommend nor support Bredon as Sir Robert Hart's successor and he knows this himself". When I expressed some doubt about it, he repeated: "It is a fact, but I rely on your honour not to quote me as your authority for it". I then asked why the F. O. had changed its mind. He said that Bredon had become very unpopular and especially throughout the Customs Service, so much so that the probable effect of his appointment would be the break up of the Service. This expression brought to my mind what your brother Jim said when I last saw him in connection with the Surinam business (Z.1348 of 7 Nov). His wife Phoebe was present at the time and these were almost his exact words: "I shall never forgive Bredon for his conduct to poor [name illegible] or for his disloyalty to the I. G. of which I have given the I. G. ample proof. If Bredon ever becomes I. G., which I think is impossible, it will 'break up' the Service, and the whole blame for it will fall upon my brother". I have heard Jim telling Kopsch and other members of the Service that the only thing that would take him back to China would be to keep Bredon out of the post of I. G. I have also heard people casually remark that after what took place during the siege, B. could never be I. G., and I have heard Cartwright say that if B. was ever made I. G. there would be a great row and scandal.

I cannot shut my ears to people's gossip, yet I do not trouble my head about it, and it is only because you put that query to me in your Z.957, that I think it my duty now to tell you something of what I have heard.

There is no doubt but that all these anxieties and worries preyed on Campbell's mind, and in February 1907 came the beginning of his last illness. A stoppage of the bowels occurred, Sir Arbuthnot Lane was called in and an immediate operation was decided upon. It all happened on a Sunday. I had been playing golf, and when I returned in the evening I was told by the doctors to go and see him before his removal to the nursing home and to ask for his last wishes in case the worst happened. I found him perfectly calm and composed and actually trimming his finger nails in order that he might appear before the nurses at his best. It was only with the greatest difficulty that

I got him to say where his papers were. He seemed chiefly concerned to let me know the whereabouts of the papers relating to the Craignish succession. My mother, sister, and I accompanied him to the nursing home and then followed an operation which lasted several hours. When it was all over, the two doctors, Lane and Stoker, came in, their faces pale and wearied, and told us that while they had not been able to do all they wanted, they thought there was a fair chance of recovery.

When Campbell recovered consciousness next day, he asked Dr Stoker whether the operation had been a success, for he must telegraph the result to Sir Robert Hart at once. Dr Stoker gave an ambiguous reply, but Campbell insisted on the whole truth being told, whereupon Dr Stoker told him that the operation had been completely successful. He was not telling the whole truth, for, as he admitted to me afterwards, he himself was aware that the operation had been only partly successful, but in the circumstances it was a justifiable deception. After three weeks in the nursing home, Campbell was brought home with two nurses and for a time made such rapid progress that he began to walk about and actually resumed his weekly letters to Hart, besides attending to some of Hart's private affairs. Then one day in May, when the sun was shining, the nurse left him alone on the balcony for a few minutes, the sun suddenly disappeared in a mist, he had a shivering fit and from that moment grew steadily worse, finally expiring on 3 December 1907.

Almost to the last he insisted on dictating a weekly letter to Hart, and right up to September came Hart's letters to him, describing the course of events in China. I have given extracts from these last letters in the Appendix.** They give an interesting picture of Hart's last year in Peking and his anxieties about the future, particularly about his successor, and they describe his last important bit of work in manning the new Customs office in Manchuria partly with Chinese officials, an entirely new development. When Hart realized that Campbell's case was desperate, however, his letters ceased, and a day or two before the end he sent a goodbye telegram thanking him for his more than forty years of splendid and faithful service.

The night before he died my father, in one of his last conscious moments, sent for me. He obviously knew that the end was near, and certain things were preying upon his mind. "I acted for the best," he pathetically murmured again and again, and then, "But the Chinese government will be generous." He was referring to his financial losses, and that brings me to mention a domestic calamity without which no record of his life would be complete. Plato, in the opening scene of the *Republic*, makes the old man Cephalus say that he is content, so far as riches are concerned, to leave his sons not less but a little more than he himself received from his father. This unhappily was not my father's lot. Like so many other able men, supremely successful in managing the affairs of others, he mismanaged and neglected his own.

He had inherited a considerable fortune from his mother and her bachelor brother; he had drawn (for those days) a princely salary from the Chinese government, to which was added many sundry allowances. Many indeed confidently anticipated that, with his salary and other emoluments and the great opportunities for making money which must have come to him in the various transactions he carried out for the Chinese government, he would die a wealthy man. He was, however, the soul of honour and from the first resolutely set his face against receiving any commission in any shape or form. One instance of this occurred when Armstrong's was building the Chinese fleet. He had a considerable holding in the firm, but, on Armstrong's obtaining the contract he immediately sold all his shares and thus deprived himself of the profit which would have accrued to him from the enormous rise in the value of the shares which occurred shortly afterwards. Similarly he refused any underwriting in the numerous loans secured on the Customs which he negotiated for the Chinese government.

His first serious loss had been in 1884, when he lost over eight thousand pounds in the Oriental Bank smash. Other minor losses subsequently occurred, but the big crash came in the early nineties. He had been unfortunate enough to get into touch with the firm of Colman and May, and as May had recently been chief cashier of the Bank of England, Campbell thought he could do no wrong in following their advice. He was induced by them to invest heavily in some American companies. All went well at first and he could have sold out at a substantial profit. But no, he held on in the hope of making a fortune for his family and of fulfilling his dream of buying back Craignish Castle; he actually ordered me out of the room when I mildly suggested that he should realize his profits and sell. A schoolboy's advice—but correct, as it turned out, for after a rapid rise the companies suddenly all went smash, and in the end he lost all and more than all, for the shares were only half paid up and he was a ruined man. I never discovered what his actual losses were, but I was given to understand that he had invested £40,000 in the various companies, so that the total loss must have been in the neighbourhood of £80,000! He bore the loss bravely and my mother never complained, but it all weighed heavily on his mind to the end. When I had to go through his papers after his death, it was pathetic to find envelope after envelope of shares containing on the outside such words as "gone to grief," "all gone," "washed away," "one of Colman and May's swindles—credat Judaeus."

As he dwelled upon his losses on his deathbed, I did my best to comfort him by saying that money was not everything, and he then muttered, "Money may come from America. The Craignish succession—all the papers at the of-fice—the story of my father's marriage with an Indian princess all a lie." He was no doubt alluding to a rich scion of Craignish who had made a fortune in America and might possibly leave his money to the head of Craignish, but I did not discover the meaning of his last words until years after when, going through the Craignish succession papers, I discovered that the opponent to his claim to be head of Craignish had sought to show that his father was mar-ried to an Indian princess at the time he married his mother, and that he had had to make inquiries to prove how utterly false this was.

I listened to all this sympathetically and then thought the time had come to give him Sir Robert Hart's farewell telegram. It had arrived two nights be-fore but we had not given it to him for fear it might excite him too much. As I read out the words "over forty years splendid and faithful service," a faint glimmer of a smile passed over his lips. It was the last earthly message he re-ceived. Immediately after he fell asleep and never woke again.

In my letter to Sir Robert, written on the day my father was buried, I said:

> You will long ere this reaches you have heard about my father's death, but I feel it is a duty I owe to you to write you a few words by this Friday mail. He died on Tuesday night last at 8:35 p. m. after a long weary illness most patiently borne and happily unattended by much suffering. We all thought after the first week that there was some chance of his ultimately recovering, but it became clear about June that there was no hope. His wonderful constitution and vitality kept him alive longer than the doctors dared hope, but during the last month he was rarely conscious. Your kind message thanking him for over 40 years

splendid service was not given to him by my mother at the time as she thought it would unduly excite him, and it was then necessary that he should be kept absolutely quiet. But you will be glad to hear that on Monday night last, the night before he died, finding him momentarily conscious, I gave him the message, and I think he understood, for just the faint glimmer of a smile passed over his face. He became unconscious again immediately after, and the nurses do not think he ever recovered consciousness, so that yours was the last mortal message that reached him. I am so glad that he got it after all.

He looked splendid after death, so calm and quiet and the features sharpened and almost beautiful. Lady Hart saw him.

Thanks to your kindness in granting him a year's leave of absence on full pay, my mother was able to provide every comfort during his illness, and Dr Stoker said that, had he been the King, he could not have been better attended.

Do not think that because I have not written to you all this time, I am not grateful for all your kindness, and I can assure you that your telegram which arrived yesterday has deeply touched us all. You too are in need of sympathy, for I know that in my father you have lost a loyal friend whom you will greatly miss.

I am sending you the little Memorial Service Book, which was used today, thinking you may like to keep it.

The letters of affection and respect for my father which my mother and I received are too numerous to quote, but Sir Robert Hart's letter to my mother was as follows:

Peking, 8 Dec. 1907
Dear Mrs Campbell,

The telegram was not unexpected, but all the same, it was a shock to read that the sufferer had passed away.

For myself personally and officially the loss is very great, and there is no replacing the departed, but this again is nothing to your bereavement, and I sympathise and mourn with you most sincerely. His vitality must have been of a surprisng quality to have held out so long after that operation, but so many months of nursing must have wearied patient and attendants and the end, however sad and regrettable, must in some measure have been a welcome relief.

We had been good friends ever since first meeting in 1863, and the work he has done for myself and China during the forty-odd years of Service life has been of rare quality and value. I shall miss him at every point but, as my own working day is also ending, the inconvenience will not be so much felt by successors starting from new points of departure. If I do live to get home again London will not be the same to me now he is gone, and, while truly sorry that the poor fellow is no more at hand, I shall regret being deprived of the talks we should have had about the multitudinous matters in which we had both been so much concerned and so much in communication. I hope his final hours were not accompanied by great pain and that he passed away in peace, but I suppose his intelligence must have also faded as his strength deserted him. Poor fellow—Heaven rest his soul! The mails due in January will probably bring me full accounts of his last moments. Meantime I have wired to the London office to continue the issue of his Leave Pay, and the Office here will take up the question of Retiring Allowance due etc., and deal with the financial part of the business as liberally as possible. Excuse me touching this in a letter of condolence and sympathy, but I hope it will be some relief to you, though it can be no consolation, to know that for the moment no pecuniary difficulty has to be faced.

In the nature of things, and after a long and useful life, it has pleased God to remove your dear husband and my dear friend, and I pray that you may be strengthened to accept what has befallen you.

With kind regards and sincerest sympathy for yourself and children, and also with real sorrow on my own account

Sincerely yours
Robert Hart

To my letter he replied on 2 February 1908:

Dear Mr Campbell,

Yours of 6 December came a few days ago.

Your father's death has quite changed everything and I am distressed in every way, grieved for family so bereaved and privately deprived of a most useful friend and associate. Thank you for the details you send, and I am specially glad my goodbye message reached him while conscious. The Memorial Service has also been received and placed where my journal recorded his death.

As you know the full pay granted for a year's leave (and which under ordinary circumstances would have stopped on death) has been allowed to be issued to the end of the period, and I am about to send a cheque for it and the Retiring Allowance due so that your mother can treat it as capital at once and invest it, instead of spending it all monthly: I think this is the best thing to do.

My own health began to fail in November, 1906, and latterly, since November 1907, I have suffered from insomnia: so I have to recognise facts and remember I am 73 and only fit to "lay on the shelf". I have applied for and got leave and expect to be in London before Midsummer. I sometimes doubt whether I shall really see London at all, for although I have had wonderful health in these four and fifty years in China, the last few weeks show me that I am about used up. I have now been "on deck" ever since I was on leave in 1878 and thirty years work—serious, heavy and continuous—without a holiday is a record: but I must now pay for it in loss of fitness, and so I make way for younger and abler men.

The Service has still some decades before it and my successor will find the post and position very big indeed and, if well handled, will make much out of both.

A great grief will be not to see your father: we would have had many talks over the doings of the last thirty years and much in common to take interest in. Now I go home almost an absolute stranger, and, as for personal acquaintances they will be few and far between.

With love to you all

Sincerely yours

Robert Hart

The only other letter of sympathy I will quote is that of Lord Rendel to my mother. He wrote:

Never have I for my part failed to keep you and yours faithfully in mind or to reckon my at one time very close relations with Mr Campbell as a memorable episode of my life. Warmth and brightness of domestic life were always your marked gifts, just as exceptional uprightness and diligence were Mr Campbell's in public service. I never met anyone more to be respected and trusted, unselfish, loyal and disinterested—in every circumstance of life. Such men cannot be replaced. When one adds to these nobler qualities his gifts of memory and power of concentration and of grasp of detail one feels more than ever that he was a man by himself. He had but one most honourable defect. He was modest and retiring to a fault.

Very sincerely and sorrowfully yours

Rendel

Hart felt Campbell's death acutely. Not only had he been his right-hand man in Europe, working quietly behind the scenes for over forty years, but he had been his close personal friend to whom he had confided his sometimes delicate private affairs. He was also trustee of his marriage settlement, and Lady Hart, who lived in England, had come to rely on him more and more for counsel and advice. It is no wonder that Hart left China shortly afterwards. He had for long been contemplating retirement but time after time had put off the evil hour. Campbell's death finally decided him. Early in the spring of 1908 he bade a sorrowful adieu to Peking and left China, nominally on leave of absence. He never returned, and he died only some three years later.

Thus came to an end a unique partnership between two men of perfect trust and understanding, a brilliant Irishman and a sober, steadfast, sturdy Scot, and China and Europe became the poorer for the loss of a link between them—a loss which was indeed irreparable, as subsequent events sadly showed.

A NOTE ON CAMPBELL'S CHINA CORRESPONDENCE

During the whole of his career as London secretary from 1873 to 1907—except for the one short interval when Sir Robert Hart came over as president of the Chinese commission for the Paris exhibition of 1878—Campbell sent a mail letter every Friday to Sir Robert in which he reviewed the political events in Europe with any bearing they might have on China. All these letters, together with Sir Robert's own weekly letters to Campbell in which he described Chinese events from his end, were carefully kept in special confidential files. The correspondence was known as the "Z" series, and how voluminous it was may be gauged from the fact that Campbell's last letter was numbered Z.1575 and Sir Robert's Z.1119. Sometime before his last illness Campbell removed all these letters to his own home, fearing they might get into improper hands, particularly as some of them contained reference to Hart's private affairs. After his death, however, on Hart's instructions, they were again moved to the London office, and there presumably they remain until this day. Should their contents ever be revealed, they would form a most interesting commentary on China and world history from 1873 to 1907. A few of Hart's letters written to my father during his last illness were not handed over, and I offer extracts from some of these below.** They give an interesting account of the revolutionary changes that were taking place in China shortly before the Empress Dowager's death.

Campbell was also constantly in communication with Lady Hart, who, after her return from China in 1882, relied entirely upon him for her business and other affairs. Campbell was trustee under her marriage settlement, and many a grateful letter she sent him. Some of her letters contain references to events in China, and of these I give some extracts.** The bulk of her letters, however, were of a private nature and were handed over to Bruce Hart by me in 1937.

In addition to his correspondence with Hart, Campbell also had a deal of correspondence with the senior members of the Service. It would be possible with these letters to construct not only a history of the Customs Service and its gradual development, but a skeleton history of China itself under the Empress Dowager, for, while personal, they naturally made constant reference to passing events. Campbell was careful to keep most of these letters, especially the earlier ones, and he also kept his own replies to them in a special green book which I handed over to the London office after his death. Here is a list in alphabetical order of the correspondents whose letters remain:

E. C. Baber, one of the British consuls in China who was employed in the commission of inquiry into the Margary murder of 1875. He later wrote some delightful books on his geographical researches in China.

Sir Robert Bredon, Hart's brother-in-law and for some time deputy I. G.

Sir J. McLeavy Brown, commissioner and for some time financial adviser to Korea

Smollett Campbell, my father's cousin, for some time in the London office and later commissioner

William Cartwright, for many years Chinese secretary at Peking and possibly the ablest man in the Service

Gustav Detring, a Prussian, for many years commissioner at Tientsin and bosom friend of Li Hung-chang; the one man of whom Hart was somewhat afraid

T. Dick, commissioner

E. B. Drew, an American, for some time statistical secretary

C. Hannen, commissioner, brother of Judge Hannen

Alfred E. Hippisley, for some time in the London office, chosen successor to Hart when the latter was thought to have been killed in the Boxer Rising

H. E. Hobson, commissioner, had charge of the coal mines in Formosa

G. Hughes, commissioner

Paul King, for some time in the London office and afterwards commissioner; author of *In the Chinese Customs Service*

Admiral Lang, organiser of the Chinese fleet

Sir Halliday Macartney, secretary to the Chinese legation in London

E. McKean, commissioner

L. Rocher, a Frenchman, commissioner, brilliant administrator

C. L. Simpson, commissioner

Finlay Smith, commissioner, brilliant mathematician

F. E. Taylor, a protégé of Campbell's and for some time in the London office; statistical secretary

INDEX

120

Franco-German War, 52, 58, 59
Freycinet, Charles de, 66, 70

Gamma, the, 42
Gas, use of in China, 12
Germany, 15, 39; and the Chinese navy,
   46, 47; and Tongking crisis, 61; loans
   from, 85; seizure of Kiaochow by, 94
Gibraltar, 1
Giles, Herbert A., 89
Giquel, Prosper, 44
Gladstone, Henry, 68
Gladstone, William Ewart, 17, 61, 70
Glasgow Herald, the, 43
Glover, George B., 52
Gomez, Barros, 75-78
Gordon, General Charles, 32, 48, 61
Gordon, Panmure, 25
Grace family, 3
Granville, Lord, 61, 63, 65; on honours for
   Campbell, 70
Granville Hotel, Ramsgate, 20
Great Britain, xvi-xvii, 5, 94; idea of
   China in, 7; and the Margary affair,
   40-42; prestige of in China, 46; and
   Tonking crisis, 61; attitudes of
   toward the Orient, 82-84; on Chinese
   loans, 85
Great Rissington, 1
Gregory, Dean, 95
Grévy, Jules, 64
Gunboats: Lay's purchase of, 8-9;
   Campbell commissioned to purchase,
   xi, 39; voyage of *Alpha* and *Beta,* 42;
   Gamma and *Delta,* 42-43; epsilon
   class, 44; iota squadron, 45; further
   additions, 48

Hainan, 45
Haiphong, 58
Hammond, 52
Hankow, 40, 90, 91
Hannen, C., 22, 115
Hanoi, 58
Hart, Bruce, 100, 114

Hart, James, 15, 23, 52, 89; on
   delimitation of frontier, 66, 78; as
   possible Inspector General, 72; on
   succession of inspector generalship,
   106
Hart, Phoebe, 106
Hart, Sir Robert, xiv, xvi, 15, 21;
   relationship with Campbell, xii,
   xvii-xviii; successor to Lay, 9;
   appointment of Campbell by, xi, 10,
   11, 43; Campbell's descriptions of,
   12, 15; and von Gumpach, 16, 17;
   London office set up by, 17-18; in
   French negotiations, 26, 28, 60,
   61-67, 68; and reform edicts, 29; and
   organization of Customs, 30-31; on
   coastal lights, 37; and purchase of
   gunboats, 40; in Margary case, 41;
   and Lang, 44, 45, 46; and international exhibitions, 52, 53, 54, 57;
   biography of, 67; attitude of toward
   Campbell, 70-71, 73; possible successor to, 72-73; offer of ministerial
   post to, 72-73; and Macao, 77; and
   J. B. Campbell, 79-80; on Sino-
   Japanese War, 82-85; on audience,
   89; and postal service, 91-92; and
   Boxers, 94, 97; rumoured death of,
   94-95; articles on China by, 96-97;
   rebuilding house of, 98-101; and
   Campbell's illness, 107, 109-110;
   letters on Campbell by, 110-112;
   correspondence with Campbell, 114
Hart, Lady, xviii, 47, 61, 82, 97; on
   Campbell's part in exhibitions, 54;
   on honours for Sir Robert, 71;
   Campbell's services to, 113, 114
Hawkes, Captain, 6
Health Exhibition, 53, 54-55
Heidelberg University, 2, 3
Hillier, H. M., 21
Hippisley, Alfred E., 21, 72, 115; on
   Tongking crisis, 59; on China after
   Sino-Japanese War, 86; during Boxer
   Rising, 94; on reorganization of
   Customs, 105

HARVARD EAST ASIAN MONOGRAPHS